INK IN MY BLOOD

My half a century in newspapers

NEIL HAVERSON

Also by **Neil Haverson**

Published by the Eastern Daily Press
in the EDP Classics series.
Available from the EDP's Prospect House office in Norwich.

Fortress H: The Early Years
Fortress H: Still Going Strong
Fortress H: The Teenage Years
Fortress H: The Aubergine Bake Repeats
Fortress H: Reigning Brats and Mogs

INK IN MY BLOOD

Ink In My Blood

My half century in newspapers

First published in Great Britain in paperback, March 2018,
by Paul Dickson, 8 Bridge Court, Fishergate, Norwich, NR3 1UE
Tel: 01603 666011
paul-dickson@btconnect.com

ISBN Paperback 978-0-9956187-4-9
ISBN Ebook 978-0-9956187-5-6

A CIP catalogue record of this book is available from the British
Library

Cover photograph by Paul Hewitt, with thanks to
John Jarrold Printing Museum, Norwich
Other photographs courtesy of Archant Norfolk, Lynn News,
Paul Hewitt and Mrs H.
With thanks to Rosemary Dixon, Librarian, Archant Norfolk.

Designed by Peter Sargent
Printed in Norwich by Interprint
www.interprint-services.co.uk

On one occasion a family commitment came into conflict with work. I didn't know what to do but my boss at the time said to me: "Family comes first. You can always get another job but you can't get another family." Wise words. I could never get another family like the one I have that has supported me through the ups and downs of life.

So this book is for Mrs H and Brats Major and Minor, I hope I have been as good a husband and father to them as they have been wife, daughter and son to me.

Foreword

Peter Franzen OBE
Eastern Daily Press Editor
(1993 – 2009)

Now you have to understand "they" were the enemy. In the newspaper world editorial and advertising had as much in common as Norwich City and Ipswich Town football supporters. It always seemed that those cash-grabbing advertising staff were selling the ground from under the feet of the editorial team who refused to be sullied by filthy, dirty money.

But instead of turf, it was newsprint over which the two sides fought. The journalists had no time for financial targets and advertising "ratios". They just wanted wide open spaces on which to write their news, features and sport content, and show off the accompanying pictures.

Not that we had anything personal against the individuals in the advertising department, but daily their wretched advertisements seem to jeopardise the plans for our content display.

The ads on the front page were strictly controlled by position and size, and so was page 3, the next show page. Advertisers always wanted "an early right hand page", because they knew this was where the eyeballs went when reading a newspaper.

So each day on the Eastern Daily Press we would tussle over the ad layout with those "nice" people from advertising and try to work out a compromise to satisfy both sides of the argument.

It was in this context I first came across Neil Haverson. Neil had an unfair advantage in these negotiations. He was such a pleasant bloke you felt guilty about trying to stitch him up. More than that, he actually understood the editorial point of view. Here was someone from the "other side" who showed empathy for what we tried to do each day – deliver a high quality Eastern Daily Press that was fair, balanced and accurate both for readers and advertisers.

At that time I should have realised here was a man who was ready "to cross the floor of the House" to eventually become a celebrated columnist for the EDP, building up a huge following of readers.

After all like most of us at the EDP, he had ink in his veins, even though it was advertising ink.

When I took over as EDP Editor, Neil's column was in its infancy and I wondered whether it could be sustained and continue to entertain the readers. But rather like Coronation Street, it was the EDP's soap opera. And the hapless Mr Haverson, Mrs H, and Brats Major and Minor became part of the fabric of the newspaper and Norfolk life.

I guess the popularity of the column was that not only was it amusing, but readers could identify themselves with many of the family situations that Neil cleverly wove with his weekly words.

Frankly there were times when I was sorry for the innocent inhabitants of Fortress H, and wondered how they felt about their daily lives being chronicled for the entertainment of EDP readers.

Neil's column has now been running for 26 years. It took a short break when the EDP was "revamped" but after a brief "holiday" is now back in the paper.

This "compendium" draws together Neil's writing over the years, and I wish him every success with the venture. This "ad-man" turned writer has truly found his vocation.

Introduction

As I wrote about my years in print I realised I simply couldn't imagine spending my working life in any other profession. The industry has an atmosphere all of its own. It's hard to put a finger on it but it wraps itself around you. Visitors to the Eastern Daily Press office sensed it and would often comment on the unique buzz.

Today the offices and production areas are populated by computer terminals on desks. At first glance it could be any major business. After all, gone are the subs tables with copy spikes and pots of glue. No picture editor holding negatives up to the light to select the best image. Reporters no longer pound away on typewriters.

The subs runner taking copy to the composing room and "running" messages has long been replaced by a computer network.

The composing room with the chatter of typesetting machines has vanished forever. And the foundry casting the semi-circular metal printing plates has been replaced by electronic output of aluminium plates.

In the Advertisement Department there were bundles of classified ads in pigeon holes, sorted into their categories. And staff drawing page plans with good old pencil and ruler.

In spite of the loss of such iconic images of a newspaper office the special buzz is still there. Trawling through my memory to compile this look back at my career has reawakened the experience of the "hold the front page" era.

I consider myself extremely fortunate to have worked in the industry when I did. I saw newspapers move from the centuries-old hot metal production to the state of the art electronic process today. And no doubt that will develop further.

The future does not look bright for the printed word, but for me, and I am sure many others, sitting in the armchair with my newspaper is simply the only way to digest the news.

In producing this book my thanks go to publisher Paul Dickson for prompting me to put down my memories. To ECN/Archant for not only allowing me access to the files for pictures and past columns, but also for providing me with the opportunity to work in the business for over 46 years.

To my good friend Paul Hewitt for coming out of retirement to take the cover photograph, and to Archant Librarian Rosemary Dixon for tracking down photographs and columns in the archives.

Special thanks, to Terry Redhead with whom I enjoyed two of the best periods of my career and who proof-read my autobiography – as if he hadn't had enough of checking my copy when we worked together.

Thanks also to the Lynn News for use of pictures of my early years.

But I must reserve my most grateful thanks for three very special people. Firstly Brats Major and Minor. They've put up with having some of their innermost secrets made public. I'm sure their street cred was severely tested when I revealed some of their escapades, particularly during their teenage years.

And of course Mrs H. She has been the main character and inspiration for the Fortress H dispatches. She has allowed me to say things about her that other husbands tell me they daren't say to their wives. In fact some have told me they wave the paper at their better halves and say: "See, that's just like you."

Her support does, of course, go way beyond the column. As the saying goes, I didn't get where I am today…

Contents

Guide to pictures in the colour section

i Hooking with a hangover: Batting after a heavy night versus the Romford Recorder on the LN&A tour in 1968.

Still single: Quentin and I pose outside St Cuthbert's Church, Thetford as we await the arrival of Miss H. Picture: Paul Hewitt.

ii Pipe dreams: I became an aspiring model for this picture taken in the late 1960s for a Lynn News & Advertiser promotional advertisement. Picture courtesy Lynn News.

ii Shades of grey: On February 16 1971 ECN trialled its first process colour printing with an advertisement in the EDP. I played the part of a husband with receptionist Christine Morley playing my wife. Mike Tubby from management accounts was the estate agent. I'm wearing brown Hush Puppies but they printed as grey.

iii Male order: Looking like something out of a catalogue I posed again in 2008 on Mousehold Heath for a feature on outdoor clothing. Picture: Antony Kelly, Archant.

iii So long to the flong: One of the last flongs to be used for platemaking at ECN. This one was for page 7 of the Eastern Evening News of September 15 1971. Picture Paul Hewitt

iv All set: The LN&A cricket team about to board the bus for the 1966 tour. Left to right: Peter Jowitt (Pedge), Pete Jenkins, Brian Kimber, the driver, Lawry Hunter, Craig Seaton, me, Neil Wiseman, Bev Bargewell, John (Sam) Hardy, Mick Sands, John Allen, John Gathercole.

iv Planning: A meeting in October 1989 when I was Admin Manager, discussing newspaper page plans. Left to right: Me, John Gardner, Jane Holbrook, Linda Bullent, Wendy Jones. Picture: Archant

v Lines of type: Invented in 1886 the linotype machine transformed typesetting enabling a small number of operators to set type for a large number of pages. Picture Archant.

vi Lucky break: A chance encounter led to my interview with the late actor Roger Lloyd Pack, star of Only Fools and Horses and The Vicar of Dibley. It turned out to be a best-selling issue for Let's Talk.

vii Battle ground: I returned to my old primary school at Downham Market in 2009 for a schooldays feature. Aged around nine I had a fight under this tree which I was actually winning until a teacher stepped in. Picture Matthew Usher, Archant

vii On air: With Nick Conrad at West Somerton recording the feature on the Norfolk Giant for Radio Norfolk. Picture Mrs H.

Bundled up: Packing the newspapers ready for dispatch at ECN's Redwell Street premises which they occupied unit 1969. Picture Archant

vii Hot off the press: One of the first editions of the Evening News to be printed in 1995 at Archant's newly built print centre on Broadland Business Park. Picture: Archant.

viii Top of the pops: With Keith Skues in the Radio Norfolk studio on the night we played the Let's Talk readers' top twenty.

viii How do you do it? Gerry Marsden told Roy Stowger and me exactly how before he went on stage at Great Yarmouth 2003.

INK IN MY BLOOD

My half a century in newspapers

I

In at the deep end

It was 3am. The sweet night air distinctive of the Fens drifted through the open van window. It took all my concentration to persuade the heavy Bedford along miles of bendy roads. A high bank on one side behind which lay a cold, dark river. On the other was a steep drop to fields of rich black Fenland soil.

I gripped the steering wheel with white knuckles as I negotiated what was then a sharp s-bend over the bridge at Brandon Creek.

Phew! Made it across the river.

Why was I doing this? After all, I was an 18-year-old trainee in the advertisement department of a local newspaper. I spent my days learning how to process advertisements for publication, delivering proofs to customers and collecting copy from the bus and rail stations. But here I was in the dead of night grappling with a van-load of newspapers on roads that can be scary to drive on during daylight.

And I'd not long passed my driving test – taken, I might add, in a Mini. I'd had a crash course in driving the van; getting used to wing mirrors as the only source of knowing what was going on behind me. I had accompanied Brian, the regular driver, on one trip in the hope of familiarising myself with the route but otherwise it was in at the deep end – and hopefully not that of the River Great Ouse.

But this was the 1960s and working practices were rather more informal; no health and safety. Had there been a risk assessment I'd never have been allowed to climb into the cab.

I was working at the Lynn News & Advertiser (LN&A), a twice weekly newspaper circulating in King's Lynn and West Norfolk; my first job since leaving Hamond's Grammar School in Swaffham.

I found one of my old school reports recently, the last one before I sat my GCEs. It must have made depressing reading for my parents. I can only imagine the concern they must have had for their son's future. Other than French, most of the teachers' comments were not optimistic about my chances of academic success.

I did manage to achieve five O Levels – but had no idea what I wanted to do with my life.

Then my father spotted an advert in the LN&A for a vacancy for a trainee in their Advertisement Department. It was a light bulb moment I – and my parents – had been waiting for. Working for a newspaper fired my imagination.

I sent off my letter, having first had it vetted thoroughly by my father. I got the job and started a career in print that was to last for the rest of my working life.

The Lynn News & Advertiser had its own composing room where the type was assembled for the paper in hot metal. Such bastions of the print industry no longer exist. Technology has advanced and pages can be produced and transmitted electronically so it's proved cheaper to centralise production.

Although the composing operation was self-contained in King's Lynn, the paper was printed at the group's headquarters in Peterborough. So the completed pages for the newspaper had to be transported 37 miles along the A47 to the presses.

Today a button is pressed and pages are output the other end as plates ready for printing. In the Sixties they got there … by bus. The completed pages were moulded in a kind of papier mache material with the delightful name of flongs. Throughout the production cycle batches of flongs were placed in large, flat wooden boxes and conveyed to the bus station by, among others, me, and put on the 336 Eastern Counties bus to Peterborough. From these, curved printing plates would be cast in hot lead.

The final flongs were taken on the Bedford van on press night.

Most of the newspapers were delivered by vans from the Peterborough plant to newsagents or wholesalers but the Lynn van would return to base via Downham Market to drop off bundles at the town's newsagents.

The regular driver was on holiday so volunteers were called on to help out. Why on earth I stepped forward I can't remember, but that was the reason a young and not too confident Haverson was weaving through the Fens in the early hours of a Friday morning.

I made it to Downham Market and delivered my bundles. At the time, as luck would have it, I lived in the town with my parents. So, around 4am, I parked up and crawled thankfully into bed. The late finish meant I could sleep in – and there was a bonus. I had the van so I saved the bus fare to work the next day.

I look back gratefully on events like that Fenland expedition. It was stressful at the time, but such a valuable experience; one piece of a huge jigsaw I was assembling as part of my lifelong career in the newspaper industry.

At Peterborough I saw the printing plates cast and bolted on the press. I watched the big machine rumble into gear and accelerate. It sounded like the London Underground and it was something that would continue to set my adrenalin running every time I watched it. The newsprint whirling through the machine and the finished newspapers spewing out the other end, tied automatically in bundles and off the conveyor to waiting vans like mine.

I also expanded my vocabulary. The reels of paper hurtled through the press at quite a pace. Occasionally one would tear; known as a web break. It appeared there were certain words, not in the dictionary, which had to be spat with venom before the paper could be re-threaded.

King's Lynn was a small operation so, even as a lowly clerk, I came into contact with all aspects of the newspaper's production.

I was involved with the editor and his sub editors in agreeing pagination and the layout of the newspaper.

I helped out in the reading room. I held the original copy while the reader read out loud from the proof, marking the typos and anything I heard that was incorrect. I learnt that when checking a football league table you read down a column of figures not across.

Reading rooms have long since gone as is evident from some of the mistakes that get through to publication. With papers having increasing numbers of pages the volume of text became so huge that reading rooms created bottlenecks in production so they had to go.

I operated the switchboard, worked on reception, delivered proofs and took down classified adverts in longhand over the phone - and did things I wasn't supposed to do in the composing room.

It was the days of powerful print unions and we non-union people weren't supposed to handle anything in the composing room. But when they were busy the compositors turned a blind eye. If I needed a proof of an advert I inked up the type, laid some paper on it and swung the roller over then slunk away with my proof. Nobody said a word.

I loved spending time in the old comp room at Lynn. I was mesmerised watching the linotype machines churning out lines of type. If ever something was invented by Heath Robinson this seven feet high clanking edifice would be it.

A magazine of matrices which are moulds for the characters, each one cut like a Yale key. Tap the letter "A" and the appropriate character would be selected from the magazine. A whole line would be typeset and cast in lead, with a long arm returning each character to its correct position in the magazine thanks to the unique cut.

Galleys, metal trays of lines of type, would be made up into pages and, along with the engraved images, locked in frames, or chases, ready to be moulded into – I do love this word – flongs.

In assembling these pages the compositors worked from the top of the page so the type was upside down and in reverse. They had the skill of reading as quickly as you or I could read it the right way round.

Of course, that's all gone now. The skill of the compositor has long since been replaced by electronic composition, often carried out by people without any newspaper experience or training. They simply have computer skills and can drop text and pictures into pre-set boxes.

Today journalists do two years of training to get their National Council for the Training of Journalists (NCTJ) certificate. In other departments a new recruit goes through an induction programme. This can be as short as a week with a whistle-stop tour around the various departments with whom they will come into contact. Two hours here, a morning there. Then it's on the job training. Within a fortnight they're almost considered old hands.

But knowledge of the nitty gritty that I learnt, amassed over several months, is not part of the curriculum.

2
A bachelor free

Working in a Sixties office was light years away from today. The dress code was one of shirt, tie and jacket. Certainly no jeans. We were yet to import the open plan office from America. Each department had its own room with just a few people in it. Now dozens share wide open spaces.

Someone sneezes, 20 people look up and a conversation starts.

Is it better to have everyone together? I'm not sure. There are pros and cons. With the close supervision it was hard to daydream in a small office, but these days it's possible to while away time by clutching the mouse and staring at the computer screen.

External distractions were limited when we cosied in a small room. It wasn't a thoroughfare so people weren't continually walking past. Mind you, we created our own internal distractions, of the like that would attract the sack these days.

Screw up a piece of paper and wrap Sellotape round and round it. You have a ball.

Complete adverts arrived ready-cast in lead tacked to wooden blocks. Take a couple of these chunks of wood and you have two bats.

A typist's chair at either end of the room with open legs front facing. You have goals.

All that was needed then was a wastepaper bin strategically placed at the door to warn of approaching management and it was game on. Whacking the ball back and forth to try to score between your opponent's chair legs.

Work was fun, the job got done – and I don't recall anybody being signed off with stress.

King's Lynn was a happy period in my life. Although, of course, when one looks back there is a tendency to view things through rose-tinted spectacles.

I left the parental home in Downham Market to move into a bachelor flat with three other pressmen. I remember that spell as carefree days. Playing our Sixties LPs on the Dansette, the odd party and evenings in the pub.

But if I think a bit more deeply, it was not all hearts and flowers. For a start, in winter it was cold! All we had was an open fire in the main living room later supplemented by a paraffin heater donated by my parents. One or other of us would often crouch in front of the grate with an open spread from an old edition of the LN&A held over the fire to draw it. Frequently the paper caught light – which was more than the fire did.

For food, the local chippy profited from our patronage as did Sidgwicks, the nearby convenience store.

Vesta Curry – remember them? – was a regular on the menu. And these days I cannot look at a tinned Fray Bentos Steak and Kidney pie without a slight heave of the stomach. I'm not sure exactly what was in them but it was an easy meal to prepare. Whack it in the oven, open a tin of peas and serve with mash. Well, not quite mash. Remember Smash? Just add water and hey presto, you had a solution of white stodge.

We were typical lads sharing a flat. We left it to each other to do the cleaning. I remember that entering the lounge there was a narrow passage of dust-free floorboards where we walked.

We had a vacuum cleaner but it had lost most of its suction and it was necessary almost to thrust the dust up the pipe.

I came home from work one evening and went straight into the front room. I heard footsteps on the stairs and assumed one of my flatmates was home. In fact, it turned out I had disturbed an intruder who had been upstairs, legging it when he heard me.

There was a front door to the three flats in the building which were on separate floors. But we had no internal front door so all the doors had padlocks. I went upstairs and found one of the bedrooms had been forced open with a screwdriver. Quentin, a reporter on the LN&A and occupier of that room, arrived home. We "bagged" the screwdriver and took it to the police station; later a detective called.

First thing he did was to spot among all the posters a street sign on the wall. It was "Portland Street" and had been found lying on the ground – in Portland Street – by one of our inmates who thought it would be a hoot to have it as a "trophy".

One of us mumbled something about it coming from Birmingham. Fortunately the detective just chuckled.

Then we went upstairs to Quentin's bedroom. The policeman let out a low whistle.

"They went through this room!" he exclaimed.

"Actually," Quentin piped up sheepishly. "It's always like this."

All they had taken was a jar of sixpences he'd been saving.

Sundays were boring. This was the Sixties and the world shut down on Sundays. Shops weren't open, no chippy and in the evening pubs didn't start serving until 7pm – and they closed at 10.30.

Often I'd go home to my parents after my Saturday sport. Not only was it something to do but I got fed well and Mum did my washing, thus saving me a trip to the launderette, something I hated.

Meanwhile, my newspaper career progressed slowly. When John, the advert clerk, moved up to become an advertisement sales representative I was promoted from sprog to look after the administration. This involved logging the ads as they were booked, planning them on the newspaper's 10-column pages and making sure the copy was in and sent to the composing room.

I liaised with the editor and the sub editors – sadly the latter are almost extinct.

I followed John in becoming an ad rep, a job for which I was wholly unsuited. I didn't have the confidence to knock on doors and make cold phone calls.

I travelled in the pool car to places such as Fakenham where we sold only a couple of hundred copies.

"How is your circulation?" one major business asked me one day.

"Maintaining," I replied enthusiastically.

He swallowed it. Perhaps I was better at the selling game than I thought.

An edict came down from head office instructing all local offices to submit the methods their advertisement representatives used to record the sales calls they made. We had no such system. After a spell of mild panic we came up with a plan. Our ad manager, Peter Jowitt (Peter Edward Jowitt nicknamed

Pedge) led the conspiracy.

Pedge purchased some record cards and a binder each to put them in. We wrote out cards for all our customers then, based on what ads had appeared in the paper, we entered details of calls. To create the illusion they had been completed over many months we used different coloured pens.

Not only did we get away with it, but so impressed with it were our masters, the system was adopted throughout the group.

3

Falling in – and out – of love

During my six years in King's Lynn I loved and lost – with the
emphasis on lost. Relationships lasted no time at all; I was soon back
with just my cricket bat or hockey stick for companionship.

I was shy when it came to women. I'd build up for ages to ask a girl out, then
babble an incoherent invitation to the pictures – or cinema as it is now called.

I did get a few dates but often fell at the "Can I see you again?" hurdle.

I'm not seeking sympathy here. Usually it was my ineptitude – except for the
time I was turned down because I wasn't tall enough.

I didn't have the gift of the gab and I would make a fist of sliding my arm
along the back of the seat to make contact with my date.

I always found it tricky when I drove a girl home. When we drew up at her
house I thought it was just too obvious to turn off the engine so I devised a
technique. When the car came to a halt, my foot would accidentally slip off the
clutch and guess what, the engine stalled. I got away with it – or so I thought.

Almost 40 years later it came back to haunt me. I wrote about this cunning
ploy in Let's Talk magazine. A couple of weeks following publication a letter
dropped on the editor's desk. It was from Angela, a lovely girl who had
worked in the classified ad department at Lynn and upon whom I used my
engine stalling routine. She remembered going out with me but not being one
of my stalling "victims."

She wrote: "I have a subscription to Let's Talk. My journey to work takes me
along a beautiful stretch of Scottish coastline and, as I prefer the bus, I can
catch up on my reading. Imagine the scene as we meander through the little
fishing villages when I come to the back page of the magazine only to find

Neil's article reflecting on his courting days prior to his marriage. I laughed out loud as I was one of the many young ladies who he accompanied to the cinema. In my case it was to see the Sound of Music, probably in 1967. I seem to remember enjoying it and, although I recall Neil had a car, I obviously didn't make the grade because I don't remember him stalling it."

Since then Angela and I have kept in touch, sharing memories of those King's Lynn days.

Eventually I could do the selling lark no more. In spite of my happy flat life, close colleagues in the office and my sporting links, I needed something with job satisfaction. Time to move on.

But where? Ink had got in my blood. I had become attached to the industry by an umbilical cord that could not be cut. A career change was not an option.

A further 40 odd miles east along the A47 in Norwich was a major regional publishing group, Eastern Counties Newspapers (ECN), producing amongst other newspapers, the Eastern Daily Press. I wrote on spec, spelling out my love of the nuts and bolts of newspapers and asking if there were any vacancies. I received a polite reply informing me they had no vacancies but my details would be put on file.

I took that as the classic "Dear John" letter. Deflated, I resigned myself to knuckling down and making the best of my existing job.

Then, a few months later, out of the blue, came a letter from ECN telling me a member of the admin staff was leaving. Was I still interested?

Was I! I replied by return and, to my surprise, the Advertisement Manager said he would come to King's Lynn and talk to me over lunch. I was impressed.

As he said later: "Well, it saved you having to have a tooth out."

I got the job and made an emotional departure from my life in King's Lynn. As you do at times like this we all pledged to keep in touch. But, as also happens, it wasn't long before I found a new life and my former colleagues got on with theirs.

I did keep in touch with my flatmate Quentin and latterly reconnected with John Allen, the assistant ad manager when I was at King's Lynn. John had stayed with the group and moved to Bury St Edmunds and became publisher of the Bury Free Press. We met regularly and often chewed the fat of our early days and lamented the decline of the industry of which both of us were so proud to be part.

Sadly John passed away in 2015 and I miss sharing with him what have become some of my most treasured memories.

I found a small bedsit in Norwich and in September 1970 I walked through the doors of Prospect House, ECN's headquarters, for the first time. I began work as an advertisement clerk on the Norwich Mercury Series, the company's group of eight weekly papers.

My new company had just moved into brand new offices. Open plan had arrived and I found myself sitting among around 30 other people. It was a culture shock after the tiny office at Lynn. Every time I left the desk I thought everybody was watching me. But I soon adapted, got to know people and lost the self-conscious feeling.

From producing three papers a week – the Isle of Ely and Wisbech Advertiser & Pictorial was also handled at Lynn – I was part of a large team looking after two daily papers, eight weeklies and other occasional publications such as the popular football paper, The Pink 'un.

I soon realised how laid back it had been at Lynn. The systems in Norwich were much more disciplined. They had to be with such a continuous publication cycle.

The papers were printed on the premises giving me bags of opportunities to get my adrenalin fix when the presses rolled.

On October 10, 1970, shortly after starting work at ECN, I joined my new colleagues to celebrate the centenary of the Eastern Daily Press. Along with the others I was presented with a commemorative mug and thanked for my contribution to the paper's success.

I must have made quite an impact in my first three weeks.

A few months later I became a model husband. The ability for newspapers to print full colour was just emerging. ECN was experimenting with the facility on its own presses. I don't know why I was chosen but I was selected to play the part of a husband to one of the receptionists. An office was rigged to look like an estate agent's and a lad from Management Accounts sat behind the desk. A full page advertisement was produced, preprinted and run in the Eastern Daily Press on February 17, 1971.

The colour was quite good but in the picture I am wearing a pair of grey Hush Puppies. They were, in fact, brown.

4
ECN, the early days

I settled into my role as features clerk, compiling and planning features for the weekly papers. On the section with me were a couple of girls looking after classified ads, a clerk dealing with the national ads booked by London agencies – and organising the company's football team – and Bill, the office manager, overseeing it all.

I have to admit that with all those people there was plenty of slack. We coped easily, but times were good. Advertisement revenues were high and there was not the pressure there is today on heavy cost-cutting.

However, things did tighten and the department was restructured. The daily and the weekly papers ceased to have separate staff and I was moved to a section called Sales Support. It did what the title suggests, support the ad sales team; taking phone calls when they were out and speaking to display advertisers who called into the office. In addition we handled all the ad features.

On the section were a couple of old hands, Bob and Roy; a features sales rep, me and another lad who moved there from the dailies ad desk. This was Paul. He and I became friends and remain so to this day. I was delighted when he asked me to be best man at his wedding to Joan.

Roy had a great sense of humour. He was a former ad sales rep who had been moved to a desk job following health problems. He had a fund of tales of his days on the road.

He told of the time he called on an antiques dealer. He said he was leaning on the leaf of a table talking to the advertiser when the leaf broke.

"Do you realise," said Roy's customer. "That table is 150 years old?"

Roy replied: "Good job it's only an old one then."

The newspaper industry is governed by deadlines. For as much immediacy as possible these were as late as practicable. The first of up to five editions of the EDP went to press at 12.30am with the final edition rolling at 3.30am.

In the morning the first of three editions of the Evening News was on the presses at 11.30am and the Late Final at 3.30pm.

That's long since changed. Newspapers cannot compete with the immediacy of electronic media so they print much earlier. In fact the Evening News is now a single edition which prints the night before publication.

In the early Seventies births, marriages and deaths announcements could be placed up to 8.30pm in the evening for the following day's Eastern Daily Press and up to 10.30am for that day's Evening News.

To cover the evening period after the working day finished at 5pm until the 8.30pm cut-off, clerks were paid extra to take down in longhand these announcements, most of which were death notices submitted by funeral directors.

I used to take parties of visitors on evening tours of the newspaper operation. Early in one tour I introduced the Advertisement Department to a group and pointed to the duty clerk. A lady at the front suddenly burst out laughing. It was my unconscious humour that amused her.

"For death notices," I had said, "we have a late deadline."

My friend Paul, who worked on Sales Support with me, was one who did this late duty, often while I worked late on a Monday to deal with weekly feature ads sent by courier from district offices.

These late duties had a diversion. Some of the roads surrounding Prospect House were used by ladies of the night. We would stand at the window and watch them plying their trade. One summer evening one of the girls had had enough of us watching from the gallery through the open window.

She strode up to the fence and invited us to get on with printing our newspaper.

At least that is the sanitised gist of what she said.

Paul and I would go for a drink when the late shift ended. He introduced me to his other friends and, thankfully, the lonely days in a tiny bedsit were in the past.

One evening I had a near-death experience. We were not on duty that night but I had arranged to pick up Paul in my car and meet friends.

I was sitting in the armchair in my bedsit when I felt a bit woozy. I stood up and my legs just buckled. I fell back in the chair. I remember wondering if it was the gas fire. Thank goodness I did. I struggled up, lurched the couple of yards to the fire and turned it off. I managed to get the window open.

I stood up again, my legs just folded and I collapsed. Luck was on my side. I fell with my nose against the bottom of the kitchen door. Air was trickling through and this revived me.

I phoned the gas board. A man came out swiftly and disabled the fire. The following day he returned and took it out to find the flue was blocked by all manner of rubble. I had been slowly poisoned by carbon monoxide.

There were no alarms in those days. Had I collapsed into the room instead of by the kitchen door, would I still be here today?

Paul was a keen photographer. He took the photographs at my wedding. He left the company after a couple of years to work in the publicity department at Boulton and Paul, a local engineering company, where he could turn his hobby into a job.

We were to work together again. Having got some experience under his belt Paul returned to ECN as a press photographer and accompanied me to take pictures for some of the Let's Talk features.

5

Moving into management

My move to the Sales Support section was the start of many. In fact over the years I had 11 jobs within the company. I managed to get a foot on the management ladder in 1982. Bill, the office manager I had worked with when I joined in 1970, retired. He had a reputation for being rather gruff but I got on well with him and found him to be a most honest and supportive manager – a rare beast!

I applied for the role and found myself in day to day charge of many of the people I had worked with in my early days. At the time, a senior manager said to me: "You can't blame that lot down the corridor anymore. You're one of them!"

The 1980s were boom years. Adverts flowed in, some days the papers contained the maximum number of pages the press could handle.

My boss, the Advertisement Administration Manager, left, and I was appointed to the role. My responsibilities extended to managing the receptionists at head office and in the districts. I was given a company car and private medical insurance. It was hard work but at least I was getting rewarded.

I got a boost early in my new role. A gripe from one or two members of my new staff was that their chairs were rather worn. I mentioned it to my boss in one of our weekly meetings. He picked up the phone and spoke to the company accountant.

"The Admin Department need new chairs," he said. "Would that help with what we were discussing yesterday?"

He put the phone down and said: "Go ahead and order new chairs for the department."

Times were so good that it was prudent to spend money rather than declare it as taxable profit.

Imagine the kudos I got when, after only a matter of days in the job, I announced that "I" had arranged for us all to have new chairs.

But the good times didn't last. As we moved into the 1990s cost control became the byword. Computerised paper planning, allocating the adverts to pages, was introduced. Fewer staff were needed so this meant redundancies among those who had been doing the job with pencil and ruler.

As a result I had the worst of Christmas presents. I was told just before we broke for the holiday that I had to make six people redundant – but I couldn't say anything. It had been decided not to spoil their Christmas so the axe should not fall until the New Year.

On Christmas Eve staff left the office saying: "Merry Christmas Neil". There were people I had worked with for almost 20 years. They were more than colleagues, but on January 2 I would have to tell six of them they had no job.

This hung over me like a black cloud for the entire festive period. On January 2, I took them into a conference room and read out a prepared statement announcing the redundancies. It was awful. Every muscle in my body was on red alert and I could feel myself trembling slightly.

I was most grateful afterwards when one or two of the staff came up to me and sympathised, saying they could see how difficult it was and didn't blame me.

Thankfully enough people volunteered to go that there was only one enforced redundancy.

While in both the role of office manager and admin manager I was often called upon to see unhappy customers in reception. I had much respect for the girls who manned the front counter. They were at the sharp end and on occasions had to deal with some really tricky people. Ads that hadn't appeared, copy that was unacceptable and, most difficult of all, errors in death announcements. They deserved support so when someone demanded to speak to a manager I always went out.

Over the years, I was threatened, sworn at and on one occasion one person roared into my face: "I'm going to pull your bloody head off!"

We called the police that time. They dealt superbly with the situation. It transpired he was mentally unstable.

For a while after that experience I was not exactly stable myself.

I must have developed a reputation for never refusing the challenge of a difficult customer. ECN was backward in recognising the gay community. We wouldn't take personal ads from homosexuals. The gay lobby chipped away but the company refused to change its policy.

One day I was at a district office when I got a call summoning me back to Norwich. The gay community were staging a sit-in in the Norwich reception. They wanted to present a petition. I was to return to base to receive it.

You may ask why, at the head office of a large newspaper group, there wasn't a single manager available to deal with the situation.

As I drove back to the office, I wondered the same myself.

Nevertheless, I headed back to the city, crept in the staff entrance and made my office ready to receive the deputation. The sit-in consisted mainly of students. Two young people, a man and a woman, were ushered into my office clutching their petition.

I explained it was company policy but I would take their case to senior management. In the course of this I made a huge mistake. I came out with a phrase that we used regularly to promote the paper.

"We're a family newspaper," I said blithely. As soon as the words were out of my mouth I knew I'd said the wrong thing.

Thankfully they were quite restrained about it. Merely asking me what on earth I thought they were if they weren't family people.

I said I would pass on their concerns and we parted on friendly terms.

The policy did, of course, change, though not, as a result of the petition.

Technology continued to move apace. My department merged with the production department. I continued to manage the planning and customer service side of things while a colleague looked after the physical make-up of the advertisements.

I was phoned at home one night just before midnight by the night composing room manager. A notoriously difficult car dealer had got through to him and was demanding to change some of the used cars in his advertisement due in the following day's EDP which was on the presses in just 30 minutes.

Goodness knows why he was still in his office at that time of night, but I phoned him and told him the paper simply couldn't be delayed. We couldn't make any changes. Out came the usual threat.

"Well, I won't pay for the ad then."

"In that case," I said. "I'll pull the ad and fill the space."

Calling his bluff worked and the ad appeared unchanged. But I waited for the repercussions in the morning. Even though he had been totally unreasonable with his request I knew the lengths we went to keep advertisers happy.

To my surprise, I enjoyed a bit of kudos for standing up to him.

The year was 1997, our children were 14 and 12. We were past the early morning pandemonium and could have a lie-in at the weekend.

We had a telephone extension beside the bed. On Sunday, September 1 it rang just after 9am. Half asleep I picked up the receiver and mumbled something unintelligible.

"Have you seen the news about Princess Diana?" demanded a voice.

It was Peter Franzen, the EDP's editor.

"We need to re-plan Monday's paper and we're bringing out a special edition later today."

By now I was fully conscious. Like many managers I knew what had to be done but had long since forgotten exactly how to do it. I phoned one of the planners and he went into the office.

On Monday morning there were congratulations all round for the combined effort that got the papers out. My sole contribution was a phone call. And I don't know if Peter ever realised he had woken me from a deep slumber.

I mentioned earlier the demise of newspapers' reading rooms. I had enormous respect for the readers. They built up a wide knowledge. If you needed to check a fact, speak to the reading room. If they didn't know, they had a reference book that would tell you.

They became familiar with such small details as dialling codes. Taking down ads over the telephone was – still is – open to error. I recall an incident where a property was for sale in Pakenham but the ad person had misheard and typed Fakenham. The reader recognised the dialling code was for Pakenham.

Of course, they were not infallible. Walk in the reading room first thing in the morning and that day's paper would be on the head reader's desk with "mistakes" marked by the editor. Anything from a spelling error to punctuation to style.

The head reader would look back on the proofs, find who had read what and speak to them.

When reading rooms were abolished we were hit with the mantra: "Right first time every time." That's all very well but we are human, and it is difficult to check your own writing. You read what you expect to see not necessarily what you have typed.

Had we had a reading room two of my classics would have been spotted. Writing about an airfield I talked of the hangers instead of hangars. And in quoting the title of a book I said it was Heroes and Heroins instead of heroines. I must have been high on something when I typed it.

The inevitable phone calls came in, and everyone thinks they are the only one who has spotted it.

Other bloomers I remember was the hotel advertising for someone to work "split shits" and the TV aerial installer who managed to slip through the wording: "For a better erection".

The most serious post-reading room errors were those in death notices. Things like "A dead granddad" instead of "A dear granddad" are extremely upsetting to the bereaved.

A measure of the distress misprints can cause is well illustrated by a call I took from a lady about her husband's death announcement. In it we had spelt Ann without an "e". I went through the usual apologies and offered to refund the money and re-run the notice.

She erupted. For fully a minute she screamed hysterically down the phone at me. I could make out not a word. Finally she calmed down said something quietly which I didn't catch before putting down the phone.

There was clearly nothing I could have done to make it right, but, perversely, maybe I had helped. Perhaps I'd given her someone upon whom to vent her grief.

We had to be alert for malicious notices. We checked as best we could but it was not unknown for spiteful people to attempt to put in a death notice for someone alive and well.

And there was the occasion when a jilted boyfriend announced the engagement to his ex-girlfriend.

At one time there was a rule that for such notices the signatures of both parties should be obtained prior to publication. Over the years such procedures were relaxed leaving the columns open to abuse.

Misprinted telephone numbers, particularly in classified adverts, have an impact beyond the inconvenience to the advertiser. More often than not the incorrect number in the paper would be that of an innocent subscriber who would get swamped with calls from readers trying to buy someone else's bargain electric fire.

We would offer a refund and/or a free ad to the aggrieved advertiser. Squaring it with the affected subscriber was not so easy. A profound apology would sometimes be accepted. Otherwise free advertising when they wanted to sell something might do the trick.

I should point out that often it was not the newspaper's fault. For adverts dictated over the telephone it was difficult to argue the case although the operator always read the details back to the caller. However, it was not unusual for customers who sent in their ads or placed them over our reception counters to give us the wrong information.

In the days before dialling codes, telephone numbers appeared with the exchange – "Telephone King's Lynn 1234". I picked up the phone one morning to find an angry woman on the other end.

"My advert has gone in with the wrong exchange," she boomed. "You've put HOMERSFIELD!"

Homersfield was delivered with such venom I was quite cowed. I said I would look into how it had happened and ring her back.

I found her original submission. I allowed myself a satisfied smile when I saw the word Homersfield in her own handwriting.

I dialled her number. Her husband answered.

"I was just speaking to your wife about the advert with the wrong exchange," I said in a voice almost quivering with anticipation. "I'm afraid she's actually written Homersfield as the exchange."

I suspect the husband was frequently on the receiving end of this dear lady's opinions.

My pleasure in making the call was far exceeded by his unbridled joy as he replied: "Oh, you can tell her!"

I spoke to the lady who was clearly sceptical but accepted my explanation. So, just to confirm things I sent her a copy of her original. I would like to have been a fly on the wall when it dropped through her letterbox.

The four cornerstones by which advertisement content is judged are legal, decent, honest and truthful. At the EDP we set the standards high but it could be difficult to explain to customers why they couldn't say certain things in their adverts.

When the Sex Discrimination Act was introduced it was confusing. We would get enquiries from advertisers asking for guidance on the Sex Act. I replied that I'd had my moments but was perhaps not best qualified to offer advice.

Some traditional job titles were now deemed unacceptable. We had ridiculous sounding jobs in the paper such as pig person instead of pigman. You could get round it by saying "Pigman, male or female".

Sometimes customers would complain in an attempt to get a free ad. Sometimes I'd speak to an advertiser and after I'd put the phone down I'd think of something I should have said that would have made my argument more convincing. On one occasion the right words popped into my mind at just the right moment.

A pub landlady phoned to complain about the ad we had published for her seeking a "Barman/barmaid". Her issue was that she had submitted the copy as "Barmaid/Barman".

I said we had merely tidied it up for continuity in our columns; a standard way of displaying job titles.

She argued that she wanted a barmaid so that is why she had put that first. I responded that you can't contrive to get around the law and did the order of words really matter? She was in the middle of a rant about it when inspiration struck.

"Look," I said. "If I came into your pub and asked for a brown and mild and you put the mild in first I wouldn't give a hoot."

She terminated the conversation immediately.

6
Bursting into print

I owe becoming a writer to the encouragement of an EDP sub editor named John Black. John assumed the additional voluntary role as editor of the then staff magazine entitled Prospect. A meeting was called to nominate a correspondent for each department to submit news from their area for the magazine. My mistake was not to attend. As a result I was designated as correspondent for the Advertisement Department. I decided to profile members of the team. A girl was a special constable, one of the lads was a martial arts expert and another girl had been on a fascinating holiday in the Far East.

When I ran out of material John said he liked the way I wrote and suggested I contribute something on general topics, not necessarily work related. Our children were still tots. I introduced them as the Vandal and the Thug and wrote about the days of nappy changing and sleepless nights. Little did I realise this was the forerunner to Fortress H.

In 1987 the weekly paper, the Norwich Mercury, was revamped. The sports editor was also my friend and neighbour Peter Steward. He wanted a light-hearted sporting column and knowing my hockey and cricketing careers together with my writing in Prospect, asked me to have a go.

Anyone who has played sport will know that as well as the serious side of playing to win there are plenty of humorous moments. I plundered my memories and wrote a column for the next three years.

This introduced Mrs H to the public as "She who lets me out to play on Saturday afternoons" with the children retaining their tags as the Vandal and the Thug.

In 1990 some market research was conducted on the Eastern Daily Press. It emerged that readers would like something light-hearted at the weekend. The EDP sports editor and another friend, Keith Peel, told me he put my name forward to the then EDP editor Lawrence Sear. Keith generously said he thought my writing deserved a wider audience.

I had a chat with Lawrie and he said I could write about anything, not just sport as I had been in the Mercury.

"We'll see how it goes," he said. "If you can't sustain it we must forget friendship and be honest about it."

I met him years later after he had left the company and the column had been running some time.

"Hmm. . . I thought it was a good idea at the time. . ." he said smiling wryly.

I did not set out to write the column as an insight into our family life. The first one was about an old Mini from our early courtship and married days. How in wet weather it had the ability to take on water like a camel. I followed it with one about a family holiday at Hemsby. This was the trend for the first few weeks.

Then one day I was walking through Wymondham. Sitting on a low wall was a girl crying. Standing in front of her was her boyfriend or husband.

"But I am sorry," he pleaded.

With a toss of the head she howled: "But you don't mean it."

This struck a chord. The next week I wrote a column that attracted the headline: "The art of male apology." In it I suggested that "you girls" aren't satisfied with an apology, you want your pound of flesh.

Letters came in accusing me of being a chauvinist. I replied in the next week's column introducing Mrs H and revealing my experiences of being in the doghouse. A week or two later I went back to a general piece. Lawrie sent it back.

"We want the usual," he said.

And so dispatches detailing life at Fortress H became the norm.

Over the years I have received many wonderful readers' letters. They reveal an underlying theme that what goes on at Fortress H is echoed in most households. Readers identify with my inability to fathom Mrs H's logic. To be accused of doing the wrong thing because "You just don't listen!" And, to return to that Fortress H dispatch that set the trend, failing miserably in the flowers and chocolates department.

I am often asked: "How do you make something up every week?"
Simple answer; I don't. Everything I've ever written has happened.
Admittedly often it's a variation on a theme.

I couldn't have done it every week if I had to make it up. Take something like
Last of the Summer Wine. In the sitcom's early days, adventures just
happened to the three old codgers. Towards the end, while millions still
enjoyed it, the adventures had become contrived. I couldn't do that.

The other regular question is: "How does Mrs H put up with it, why is she
still married to you?

Indeed as I look back, I wonder, would she have married me if she had
known our family life would be made public weekly for more than 26 years?

I must say that she and Brats Major and Minor have been terrific sports to
have some of their personal secrets in print. I do think the children basked a
bit in the reflected glory and I think Mrs H gets quiet satisfaction when people
meet her. EDP readers have formed the impression that she is a rather large
woman wielding a rolling pin – can't think why. In fact she is slim and petite.
She delights in telling people: "You shouldn't believe all you read in the
papers."

She does read it every week before it is published and always has the power
of veto. She rarely changes anything beyond punctuation, phraseology and
grammar.

I say she reads it every week, in the very early days she didn't.

She says: "It wasn't even on my radar when it first started until the head
teacher at the first school said something to me and laughed. I didn't know
what she was talking about but I laughed along.

"Then I went into the local post office and the postmaster did a Nazi salute
and said: 'Ah ze Fuhrer.' I looked behind me to see who he was talking to –
but it was me. When I mentioned it to Neil he said it must be because of
something he had written in the paper. Ever since then I read it every week so
I know what he is telling everybody."

In sharing our lives with EDP readers, I have produced a diary. A weekly log
of our children growing up and of marriage to Mrs H; the love of my life, my
best friend and confidante.

Now in retirement we can look back at those columns and enjoy so many
memories. Memories that might have otherwise gone into the brain's recycle
bin.

7

Launching Let's Talk

For 15 years I was writing firstly in the Norwich Mercury then the EDP while maintaining full-time employment as part of the commercial operation. Being in the right place at the right time is often the happy coincidence that can change your life. So it was for me in April, 2002.

I was approached in the gents' toilet.

I happened to be in there at the same time as Bob Crawley, a senior editor.

"Ah," he said. "We want you to write a column for a new magazine. We're having a meeting, I'll let you know where and when."

I went along and found I was part of a project, code-named Silver Fox. This was the initial planning meeting for a new magazine to be called Let's Talk, aimed at the older reader.

Rather than just writing a column I became part of the whole process. In July that year I was seconded two days a week to work with the launch editor, Terry Redhead, who was to become a close friend and colleague.

We pulled together the content for the first issue scheduled for October, 2002. I had done the odd bit of "reporting" for my columns but this was my first foray into journalism, and I must say I loved it! For the launch I was put on the project full-time.

The company had said it would publish the magazine for three months and if it looked "to have legs" it would continue producing it for a year, then review it.

We hoped the first issue would sell 10,000 copies and that we could push that up to 15,000. It sold more than 32,000. I was told to stay with the magazine, and so a whole new career opened up for me.

After three months, Terry moved back to his day job, and a new editor was appointed – another good friend, Roy Strowger – and I became chief writer.

There were a couple of changes of editor, then in 2009 there were some savage staff cuts throughout the whole editorial department. Of the four editorial staff working on Let's Talk, three were made redundant, leaving just me plus Paula, the advertisement sales representative. Somehow, between us, we kept the magazine going. By default I became editor. I took the opportunity to make some small changes I had always wanted to see implemented and happily the magazine survived.

A production editor was then appointed and Let's Talk carved out a niche in the market with a very loyal readership.

In 2012 I was due for retirement. I went to the boss and announced the time had come. She asked me if I wanted to stay involved. Of course I wanted to, but I had been building up to retirement and I needed to discuss it with Mrs H.

She had always had concerns over my retirement. I didn't have any real hobbies and she wondered what I would do with myself. So when we talked it over she was, as ever, supportive of me and we agreed I should stay on.

It was decided I would do three days a week – but who would do the other two?

As part of the 2009 cull, Terry Redhead, with whom I had worked to launch the magazine, had been made redundant. I was horrified, as were many others, that a senior journalist of Terry's calibre could be let go.

Terry and I kept in touch, meeting regularly for lunch. I kept him up-to-date with company gossip and he told me how he was getting on in his new career as a freelance writer and gardener.

However, as often happens when staff are cut, some areas found themselves under severe pressure and, following a change of management, Terry was brought in part-time to help sub-edit the Great Yarmouth Mercury.

I mentioned to him I was going to scale down to three days a week. He said immediately he would do the other two days.

So the original team was reunited. It worked perfectly and we went on to co-edit Let's Talk for more than four years.

But finally it was time to hang up my keyboard. And on December 30, 2016 I left the company I had been with for more than 46 years.

Undoubtedly my last 14 years on Let's Talk were the best of my working life. Writing local features took me into readers' homes. It never ceased to amaze me the fascinating stories that so many "ordinary" people have to tell – and they had no idea how interesting they were.

The lady who walked across Germany during the war to escape the Nazis. The remarkable lady who travelled the world nursing in such places as the Belgian Congo, Australia, New Zealand and Hong Kong. She travelled on Cunard's great ocean liners, including the Queen Mary's maiden voyage following refit after war service. I spoke to her when she was 92 and she had crystal-clear memories of helping with the harvest in her home village of Wendling in Norfolk.

I was interviewing an entertainer from west Norfolk about his life and times on stage. He casually dropped into conversation that he was the very first person to appear on the TV soap, Crossroads.

Apparently the opening scene of the first episode had a Mini draw up outside the hotel. He told me it was pushed on from the side. His starring role was to get out and walk through the doors into Crossroads Motel's reception.

A colleague, Chris, from another department, had once worked for an agency where he led a team that coined the AA's slogan: "The fourth emergency service". I wrote a feature on the AA's 75th anniversary. Their press office arranged for an AA man to come to Prospect House to be photographed and interviewed.

Paul took the photographs and then I took the AA man to the staff canteen to interview him over coffee. As we started he said: "Do you know, sometimes I sit on the cliffs at Sheringham and the lifeboat men come after me and say: 'Fourth emergency service?' what about us?' I'd like to meet the person who came up with that."

"Stay right there," I said.

I rushed up a flight of stairs, along the corridor and grabbed Chris.

"Got someone who wants to meet you," I said breathlessly.

I introduced them and left them together for a few minutes. It was if it had been planned.

I am sure any feature writer would say one of the joys of writing such articles is the opportunity to have a go at a variety of things. I've been ballroom dancing, Canadian pony riding and cooked cheese scones for the National Trust at Willie Lott's cottage in the Dedham Vale. I've been hypnotised, had laser treatment on my face and had sessions of the Alexander Technique.

Sadly it didn't improve my posture.

We produced a fascinating series of "Then and Now" features. Among other professions I looked at were the police, the ambulance service and doctors. For a feature on teachers I visited my old primary school in Downham Market. That was real lump in the throat stuff.

For many of the features I was accompanied by one of the Archant photographers. They are masters of their craft. If ever I had to take the pictures they were flat and unimaginative, whereas the professionals I worked with could sum up the scene in seconds and create the perfect shot. Also, of course, their equipment was far superior to my point and shoot.

One memorable occasion was with cameraman Ian Burt. Ian is an intrepid photographer. He took the photographs for a feature I did on tenpin bowling in King's Lynn. I asked Ian if he could put on his zoom lens and get a close-up of a bowl shattering the pins.

"Right," he said, but didn't reach for his zoom lens. The bowlers were using the outside lane so Ian marched along the edge to within around six feet of the pins. Flat on his stomach he draped himself over the side of the lane and shouted for the bowler to let fly.

My whole body was tense as I watched the bowl whistle down the lane. It fizzed past Ian's left ear and struck...the pins – and he got the shot.

The feature that stands out for me above all goes back to the edition of January, 2003. I compiled a special on the 50th anniversary of the 1953 floods. Speaking to people from Hunstanton to Lowestoft who lived through that awful night of January 31, 1953 I heard stories of devastation, loss of life and amazing heroism.

In the extensive EDP photographic archive I was able to find dramatic pictures of many of the scenes involved in the stories I was told.

Within 24 hours the sea breached the east coastline in 2,000 places killing 100 people. More than 5,000 homes were destroyed and countless animals perished.

I spoke to Ann Proprdan, who was 18 when the water engulfed Snettisham. She was with her mother Emily in their wooden bungalow when water began bubbling under the door. They climbed on furniture. Their heads were on the beams when thankfully the water stopped rising. A side of the bungalow fell out and they managed to swim on to the roof.

Emily wanted her handbag. Incredibly, Ann dived under water into the kitchen and retrieved the handbag together with her father's overcoat.

Wrapped in the coat they clung to the chimney.

They were rescued by Noel Linge and his father, who got ropes, tied them to telegraph poles and inched their way forward. They came across Ann and her mother around midnight. They were taken to the Church Hall, where the doctor said if Noel had arrived just 15 minutes later they would not have survived.

And there was 17-year-old Arthur Driver. Helping to search beach huts he came across three sisters. Two were dead, the other died later. Arthur's parents had gone to Hunstanton to check his grandparents were safe. Tragically they had both drowned. He was matter of fact about it when he recounted his story.

"I had time off for the funeral, but when you're 17 I suppose it's all one thing and another."

In contrast Red Cross leading stretcher bearer Tommy Mickleburgh told me: "Arthur was the real hero. He was only a lad and had never seen a dead body before. He deserved a medal."

These are just two of the stories I heard that made me realise the scale of what Mother Nature unleashed on unsuspecting communities.

8
Seeking out celebrities

I was lucky enough to interview a number of celebrities. When I started on Let's Talk I hadn't had much experience of doing this. To see how it was done, I went with then editor Roy Strowger to Great Yarmouth to interview Gerry Marsden, of Gerry and the Pacemakers. I remember we walked through the theatre with Gerry and his roadie to the dressing rom. The first thing the roadie did was to open a bottle of wine for Gerry to have a drink before he went on stage.

Gerry was a very amiable fellow and insisted the roadie took a picture of him with Roy and me. He didn't offer us a glass of wine though.

There was charming former cricket commentator Henry Blofeld. I heard his booming voice long before he came into the room.

Penelope Keith of The Good Life. Frosty, at first, she mellowed towards the end. I learnt later that she doesn't like the media.

Brigit Forsyth, Thelma in The Likely Lads, was lovely. I said to her: "You know what I'm going to ask you about next."

"Go on," she chuckled. "I don't mind". Not all celebs are happy to talk about the part that made them famous.

One of my favourite interviews was with Liza Goddard. Liza was on the cover of our first issue in October, 2002. She lives locally so was a perfect celebrity for the launch. I didn't do that interview but in 2008, when she was in the pantomime at Norwich's Theatre Royal, we wanted her on the cover once again.

I met her at the Hawk and Owl Trust at Sculthorpe Moor. At the time she

---

was president of the Trust; she is still a trustee.

I spent a couple of hours with her and her husband wandering around the delightful nature reserve. She was warm and easy to talk to – and quite unfazed as photographer Ian Burt leapt around her taking his pictures.

From football there was former England and Norwich City players Martin Peters and Maurice Norman.

Was it a goal? I asked Martin Peters of the famous strike in extra time in the 1966 World Cup final.

"Yes," he said. Then added, to my disappointment: "At least I think it was."

And one of my most treasured memories is spending a glorious summer's afternoon in the delightful garden of Maurice Norman's secluded Suffolk cottage. With us was Maurice's wife Jaqueline. Maurice produced corned beef sandwiches and I sat there enthralled by his tales of growing up in Mulbarton, and playing for Norwich before joining Spurs, where he was part of the famous 1961 double winning team. And of course his England career, where he would have been in the victorious World Cup squad had he not broken his leg. Jackie Charlton took his place.

I told Maurice I watched the first ever game under floodlights at Carrow Road. The Canaries played Sunderland, but lost 3-1. Maurice informed me that it was thanks to him that game took place. He had been sold to Spurs to pay for the floodlights.

I still keep in touch with Maurice and Jacqueline and we often mention that sunny afternoon and corned beef sandwiches. I remember saying at the time: "This is supposed to be work!"

To get a celebrity for an interview is not easy. Often you have to go through an agent. These people act as gatekeepers. If you can get past them the celebs are usually fine, especially if they want to promote a book, an album or a show they are appearing in locally.

With Roger Lloyd Pack, of Fools and Horses and Vicar of Dibley fame, the opportunity rather fell into my lap. Mrs H and I went to a concert one Saturday evening that was part of the Holt Festival. We were queuing to go in, wearing our coloured wristbands which confirmed we had paid.

A steward came down the line saying: "Don't forget your wristbands."

A voice behind me said: "Where do you get them from."

I turned and immediately recognised Mr Lloyd Pack. I pointed to a tent and, as he headed off, he said: "Please hold my place in the queue."

He returned a few minutes later with his wristband – and clutching a pint of beer. His wife joined him and we chatted amiably as the queue moved forward.

You cannot imagine how hard it was for me not to burst out: "I wanna interview you for my magazine."

But I contained myself. It wouldn't have been fair when he was on an evening out with his wife.

On the Monday morning I emailed his agent requesting an interview, adding: "Tell him I was the one who kept his place in the queue on Saturday evening."

Roger himself emailed back, saying: "I guess I owe you something."

The interview was arranged at his north Norfolk cottage. I organised a photographer to come with me to get a good shot for the front cover.

We arrived at his home tucked away in the countryside to find him dressed down. He had on an old pair of cords and a scruffy woollen jumper.

The photographer did his best. Back at base they said: "You can't put a picture of an older man in a baggy old jumper on the front cover."

But I did – and we had the biggest sale of the year.

There is a postscript to the story. Following publication I received an angry email from Roger Lloyd Pack. He said I had given away where he lived, something I had promised not to do.

I re-read my copy and emailed, pointing out that I had said nothing more than he lived in north Norfolk. Exactly what we had agreed.

The interview was picked up and repeated in the Eastern Daily Press, and he replied saying well, it must have been in the EDP.

I sent him a copy of the EDP version, which was simply a repeat of what had appeared in Let's Talk.

His reply was somewhat contrite. He admitted he hadn't noticed it but had been told by someone it was there.

He said he should have checked before firing off an email and ended saying he was pleased with the feature and: "No hard feelings."

9
On the airwaves

As part of the launch promotion for Let's Talk I went on BBC Radio Norfolk to talk about the magazine and its aims. Thereafter I had a spot every month to chat about the latest issue. I was on air with a number of the presenters, including Louise Preist, Roy Waller, Stephen Bumfrey and, of course, the station's then editor, David Clayton. David became a contributor for Let's Talk with his monthly look at classic motoring and stars of the past.

I have the utmost respect for these presenters. When I write something I can reread it as many times as I like before submitting it for publication. Once a presenter says something it's out there. No second chance

I can sit and stare out of the window when I'm lost for inspiration. Presenters have to think on feet and avoid "dead air time".

I did some specials for Radio Norfolk with Nick Conrad. I went to West Somerton with him to record a feature on the Norfolk Giant, Robert Hales. I am supposed to be related to Hales somewhere on my mother's side. I am almost two feet shorter than my ancestor. Clearly, I didn't inherit those genes.

Nick and I visited Robert Hales' grave and went in the church. He left me with the microphone to record a few minutes' audio. It's not easy to talk fluently for two minutes without umming and erring.

I'll stick to the keyboard.

A reader sent me a copy of an American magazine, "Living in the West", aimed at senior citizens which had printed an old photograph of Felixstowe. I emailed the editor to say I was editor of a similar magazine in the UK.

The next thing I knew the editor rang me to say she was in Suffolk and could we meet? It turned out she was originally from Ipswich. We met and as a result she wrote a memory piece for Let's Talk. For a year or more I wrote a column for her magazine regaling her readers with tales of real ale, stately homes and our quaint way of life.

Nick Conrad arranged for a call to the States and we recorded a fascinating programme with the editor and her production manager.

We ran a poll with former pop pirate Keith Skues, to find out readers' top 100 tunes of the Sixties and Seventies, and asked the reasons why they chose them. Keith and I played the final top 20 on Radio Norfolk on one of his late-night Sunday shows, finishing with the number one around 1am in the morning.

Readers were supposed to vote for an individual record from those decades. The top tune turned out to be Unchained Melody. What we didn't spot was that readers voted for recordings by two different artists; Jimmy Young in the Sixties and The Righteous Brothers from the Seventies, so it wasn't really a worthy winner.

But after more than 52 years in the industry, 46 plus at ECN/Archant I still can't quite let go. I still write my whimsical Last Word in Let's Talk and the Fortress H dispatches have been relaunched fortnightly in the Eastern Daily Press.

I haven't quite hung up the keyboard yet.

10
Public speaking

I was invited to speak to clubs and societies. Standing on my hind legs in front of people was rather daunting, but I decided to have a go. I'm glad I did. The groups were always welcoming, particularly the Women's Institute. They are a warm and hospitable bunch. I got plenty of valuable feedback about the magazine and always a cup of tea and a piece of homemade cake at the end – after I'd judged that month's competition.

At one talk, I was sipping my tea with one of the members.

"I'm glad you've seen us and all the things we do," she said purposefully. "People think we're a jam-making club."

At that point the president banged on the table and announced: "Ladies! Just a reminder that next week Mrs Jenkins will be telling us how to make lemon curd."

You couldn't make it up. My tea-drinking companion fell strangely silent.

As a theme for my talks I chose the history of the Eastern Daily Press. I had squirreled away papers over the years and had built up a small library which charted the changes in the newspaper from 1970.

But I decided to research the paper back to its launch as the Eastern Counties Daily Press in 1870. I found some fascinating facts.

Inflation was almost non-existent. It was not until 1915, 45 years after the paper was first published, that staff got a wage rise; two shillings due to "rising prices".

Three years later came the first cover price increase, from a penny to a penny-halfpenny.

A frequent question was: why is there often bad news on the front page? Simple answer is that it sells newspapers. To illustrate this I recounted the story of the Thorpe rail disaster, which occurred on September 10, 1874.

The London to Yarmouth express was due in at Thorpe Station at 9pm but did not arrive until 9.15. A passenger train was sitting at Brundall waiting for the express to pass.

Inspector Alfred Cooper, a man of 15 years' service, was concerned about the delay and suggested to Station Master William Sproal, the Brundall train should go early.

Sproal said: "We'll get her off," meaning the express.

Cooper misunderstood him and assumed he meant the Brundall train. He telegraphed at 9.26 and the Brundall train set off at 9.31. He then saw the express pull out. He telegraphed to try to stop it, but he was too late.

At 9.45 the trains met head on at Thorpe Gardens. Both were at full speed, around 25 miles per hour. The drivers and firemen died instantly. In total, 27 people were killed.

Cooper was found guilty of manslaughter and given eight months' hard labour. Great Eastern railways paid out £40,000 in compensation.

For two days the circulation of the EDP went from 2,000 to 20,500. Such was demand, on Saturday, September 12 the paper had to reprint the previous day's report as well as the updated news.

A post script to this story is that a second set of tracks had been laid which would have avoided the disaster. They hadn't been brought into use because they were awaiting…a health and safety inspection.

11
And then I met Mrs H

In the early Seventies the Advertisement Department at Eastern Counties Newspapers boasted a typists section. Three ladies typed letters, reports and operated the Gestetner, that old-fashioned duplicating machine.

I became friendly with one of them, Miss L and her friend Miss H, who worked in the Market Research Department. We'd meet in the canteen for lunch. Then, the one from the Research Department, Miss H, announced she was moving flats. I volunteered to help her move – even though I only had a Mini. Fortunately young flat dwellers travelled light in those days.

I arrived at her flat and we loaded up the car and set off to her new accommodation, a temporary arrangement with a friend until she found somewhere permanent. When we arrived, I heaved her small bookcase from the car. The books were still in it, making it rather heavy.

"Right," I gasped. "Where's it got to go?"

I followed her finger as she pointed to a block of flats – upwards. ("Oh, didn't I tell you?") I lugged that wretched bookcase up I don't know how many flights of stairs. Red-faced with eyes bulging, I made it to what turned out to be the top floor.

Miss L and Miss H found a house together on Dereham Road, Norwich. It was 1972, the year of the power cuts. These were on a rota and we found that, for example, if my area lost electricity at 6pm, the girls' would come back on. So, whoever had power after work would cook the tea. Usually we ate at the girls' house as it was more salubrious than my tiny bedsit.

On one occasion I cooked a whole load of sausages before the power went off and dashed to Dereham Road where the girls had made a trifle for dessert. If their power went we dined by candlelight in front of the flickering fire.

We became good friends. Miss H and I became particularly close. Romance blossomed and she moved in with me. The relationship progressed and we decided to get married.

Miss H phoned her mother and said: "We're getting married as soon as possible. I'm not pregnant! We just don't want a lot of fuss."

St Cuthbert's Church in Miss H's hometown of Thetford was booked six weeks ahead for April 7, 1973. Miss H became Mrs H. It was the only date in the hockey season when there was no fixture. I maintain to this day it was just a happy coincidence. I'm not sure if my bride wholly believed me, then or now.

As she arrived at church on her father's arm, the photographs show storm clouds gathering in the background. Could it have been an omen?

In the Grand National that year there was a horse running named April 7th. Surely if ever there was a dead cert this was it. At the last minute the horse was withdrawn from the race. Another omen?

I can't remember much about the marriage service other than an incident following the first hymn. At the rehearsal the vicar, the Reverend Jones, said to Miss H: "When we come to the marriage vows and I put my hand out I want your right hand. If you offer your left I will ignore it."

This was clearly something that she committed to memory. As the sounds of the organ died away from the first hymn the Reverend Jones put out his hand. Remembering her coaching Miss H's right hand shot out and gripped the hand of a surprised vicar.

He hissed: "I just want to take your service sheet!"

Extravagant weddings weren't so much the thing then. Miss H's mother organised the catering at a local village hall. Surrounded by friends and relatives it was a warm and informal reception.

My best man was my former King's Lynn flatmate, Quentin. He helped me hatch a plan for our getaway from the reception. He would drive us off in his car as if he was taking us on our honeymoon. In fact my car was parked out of sight a short distance away.

As we clambered into his car several guests hurled quantities of confetti at us, most of which ended up in poor old Quentin's car. As a result he had a clean-up job whereas we escaped in a car without the traditional ribbon, graffiti and tin cans in tow.

Quentin lives in Canada now. I don't think this incident prompted him to emigrate.

He contributed a magical moment to our honeymoon. He had wheedled out of me where we staying for the first night; The Bell Hotel at Clare in Suffolk. He insisted he wasn't going to do something silly like cancel the reservation. I trusted him.

When we were checking in at the hotel the receptionist said there was a message for us. She handed us one of the hotel's postcards. On it Q had written: "To add a bit of sparkle to your marriage."

He had driven to Clare and paid for a bottle of champagne to await our arrival. What a wonderful gesture!

But it almost caused our first disagreement.

"Would you like it in the bar or in your room?" asked the receptionist.

"In the bar, I think," I replied.

"In our room," said Mrs H.

We had it in our room. I was overruled. Was this a sign of things to come?

She was, of course, right, it was far more appropriate. We sat by the window in the twilight sipping our bubbly and replaying our special day. It was a magical moment and we are grateful to Q for his thoughtfulness.

For our honeymoon we toured southern England staying at B&Bs. By Thursday the money had run out and we returned to Norwich to start married life.

And by happy coincidence we had a hockey match on the Saturday.

At that time neither of us particularly wanted a family. But perspectives change and 10 years later our daughter was born at the old Norfolk & Norwich Hospital. Any father who has witnessed a birth cannot fail to have been moved by the experience and come away with unbridled admiration for the way women deal with it.

I still have what I call my maternity jumper. It is squirreled away as one of the reminders of that landmark occasion. Every time Mrs H had a contraction she grabbed me by the jumper and pulled hard. I ended up lying across her as if we were wrestling and I was going for a submission.

The arrival of Brat Major had one scary moment. As soon as the cord was cut a nurse spirited her way. We learnt later that she had meconium in her lungs and this needed to be cleared out. There was no lasting damage but things were tense for a while.

As Mrs H lay there recovering our new daughter jibbered away in a cot. A nurse arrived with toast for the exhausted mother.

"It's not for you," she said to me rather tartly.

I was starving! It was midday and we'd been at the hospital since 3.30 in the morning. When the nurse's back was turned, generously, Mrs H let me have a small square.

Two years later Brat Minor was on his way. He was born at the old Drayton Hall Maternity Home. The one thing that sticks out in my mind was sitting in the waiting area while Mrs H was undergoing some checks. Suddenly I became aware of the most horrific screaming.

Blimey, I thought, she's going through a difficult birth. Then I heard the words: "Tonight on BBC 1…"

It was the telly.

In those early years Brat Major was a handful. She wanted to be involved in everything; full of energy she was always on the go.

My mother came for a couple of days to look after her while Mrs H was at the maternity home having Brat Minor, and I was at work. Of Brat Major she used to tell us: "You ought to square that girl up."

But when we arrived home with our new-born son, Mum was exhausted. She was led away almost trembling.

"She knew everything," she exclaimed wide-eyed. "She told me where things were kept and said: 'Mummy doesn't do it like that.'"

She offered no further advice on our parenting skills.

I arrived home from work one evening to be met by Mrs H at the front door clutching the young Brat Major. I had barely crossed the threshold before she thrust our daughter into my arms with the words: "Here you are, I've had her all day, now you can have her."

One day, when Brat Major was just a toddler, the postman knocked on the door and said: "Do you know your daughter's climbing out of the bedroom window?"

Mrs H's feet barely touched the stairs. She found her daughter had assembled bits and pieces to get on to the window sill and was on her way out of the up and over window. We think she had seen the cats climb up there.

But you never get two the same. Brat Minor was much more laid back. Give him a toy car and he would amuse himself for ages. Whereas his sister insisted on doing everything for herself – choose what clothes to wear and dress herself – Brat Minor wouldn't even try. He'd just sigh and say wearily: "Can't do it Mummy."

That's not to say raising him was trouble-free. I arrived home from hockey one Saturday to find the lower pane of glass in the front door had been replaced by a piece of hardboard. Apparently he had been zooming around on his ride-on Thomas the Tank Engine. Steaming down the hall he had failed to negotiate a sharp right hander into the living room and careered into the front door.

It was an expensive repair but thankfully neither he, nor Thomas, were damaged.

As he got older and became interested in electronics I drilled holes in various walls for cables; the evidence of some of these is still visible today.

Aerials were erected on outside walls so he could talk to people around the world on his amateur radio.

There was the occasion we had blocked guttering above his bedroom window. It turned out to be a metal money box with a wire attached to it. He had climbed on to his window sill and, dangling precariously over a concrete path, somehow reached up to lodge the money box in the guttering to act as a make-shift aerial.

It was on September 8, 1990, when they were seven and five years old, tales of their growing pains went public with the launch of the Fortress H column in the EDP.

12

Sporting life

My mother would often say: "Sport opens doors." She meant that through local sport you would meet a whole variety of different people. People who might well be able to help you in life. These days it's called networking.

And Mum was right. Sport took me all around Norfolk. I did indeed meet many people, and later in life I came across a number of them in the course of my career.

Also, by playing cricket and hockey around the county I can find my way to some of the remotest parts of Norfolk.

My father had been stationed as a police inspector at Swaffham and played cricket for the town. I played for my school, Hamond's Grammar. It was natural for me to join the town's team. It was the era of the village green game. No leagues, no importing players to boost results. Most players lived locally – and it wasn't all about winning. It was also about fun.

I played on some of the most delightful of grounds. At Sandringham, the pitch behind the church. Also tucked away on the Queen's estate was the home ground of Hillington and Flitcham. And of course the picturesque ground at Anmer. To get to it involved going through a farmyard and a field and we played in front of Anmer Hall, recently the home of the Duke and Duchess of Cambridge. Sadly the club folded some years ago but like me it must have left fond memories for many a local cricketer of the Sixties.

Other grounds I remember include Bradfield, Toftrees and Grimston where I see the tree that used to be a few yards in from the boundary has finally been removed. If you hit it, it counted as a four.

Hockey too was a different game then. Played on grass, no artificial pitches, and again no leagues. Just playing for the hell of it. We didn't need the incentive of league points to have a ding-dong with the likes of Harleston Magpies.

When I first played against them at their Weybread ground we changed in some nearby farm buildings. Later we were upgraded to the pub, The Heath House. A number of the Harleston team were farmers and I seem to recall the strength of their team depended on what was going on agriculturally at the time.

Today they boast a smart clubhouse, two artificial pitches and several teams – both men's and women's.

The other doors sport opened were pub doors. A pint after the game was an important part of the package. The Ffolkes Arms at Hillington was a west Norfolk watering hole. There was The Plover at Thetford or perhaps we'd stop off at the White Horse at Little Cressingham on the way home.

The Lynn News & Advertiser was a cricketing office. We had our own works team and everyone in the department where I worked, played. The company owned the adjacent building which, for a time, was empty. It had a long corridor, just the right length for "net practice".

We found an old door in the yard. We laid it across an oil drum; hurl the ball at the flat surface of the door to be snapped up by someone the other end. We had made a slip cradle to practise catching.

Such was our enthusiasm for office games, we broke a window. As the office junior I had to take one for the team. I was blamed for throwing a ruler around. I was admonished and a glazier was called.

Trouble was, we did it again – and again. The window was made up of individual small panes. Rather than own up we bought a supply of glass cut to fit, some putty and tacks, and carried out our own repairs.

We played on Wednesday evenings, against many of the local clubs I played against on a Saturday for Swaffham. As soon as work was finished it was off to Limberts fish and chip shop for a feed before we took to the field.

Afterwards, the post-match analysis in the pub. During one of those sessions someone floated the idea of a cricket tour. The suggestion was met with hearty support – support that, surprisingly, was still there the following day once the effects of the beer had worn off.

I took on the task of arranging it. I telephoned newspapers in other parts of the country and managed to arrange some matches against local papers in Kent, including the Kent Messenger, now owned by my old company, Archant.

We arranged accommodation and hired a minibus. The driver was to be Brian, the regular driver of the Bedford van for whom I deputised in my early days with the paper.

It was such a success we organised more tours. We headed west and took on the Leamington Spa Courier, followed by the Oxford Mail.

These tours were typical male bonding weekends. As you would expect, plenty of ale was consumed over the three days. In Oxford we hired boats and rowed up the River Isis – to a pub.

And on the field there was the common denominator that we and the opposition worked in the same industry and the games were played in the best of spirits.

We clearly demonstrated we were having a good time as the Leamington Spa Courier arranged a reciprocal tour to Norfolk.

On one tour we visited Romford. We arrived the evening before and, following a wander around the town, settled into our hotel with a few ales.

I had a few too many and to a crowded bar imparted my views on the local female population I had spotted on our tour of the town.

"I've never seen a town stacked with so much bloody crumpet!" I slurred.

I did have vague memories of saying it, but even if I hadn't, my teammates reminded me of it the following day and for weeks afterwards.

As a result of my overindulgence, the next day I was the worse for wear before the game, unlike my fellow tourists who headed to the bar for a liquid lunch before we played. Here I can vouch for the old adage, hair of the dog. While I couldn't look my usual pint of bitter in the mug, I battled through a half of mild. To my amazement, my metabolism reacted positively and I managed to bat and keep wicket that afternoon with a modicum of success.

When I moved to Norwich I joined Carrow Cricket Club. It was the works team of Colmans, the mustard people. They ran two teams but didn't have enough employees who wanted to play so took on associate members.

Home games were played at Lakenham, the absolute Lord's of Norfolk. It was also Norfolk's Minor Counties home ground. It was a treat to change in the historic thatched pavilion and play on a pitch that could have doubled as a bowling green.

From the days of village grounds where a firm off drive could get hung up in the long grass well before the boundary, I had moved to seeing a gentle forward prod race for four.

Also, I was introduced to another batch of grounds I hadn't played on before such as Ingham, Bradfield and Denes Oval at Lowestoft.

Now, if you wear glasses as I do, the Denes is not the place to play when the wind is blowing off the sea. Batting with a film of salty mist on your lenses ensures you won't be at the crease very long.

But my days of friendlies were over; it was league cricket and the tone of the game changed. A shoulder injury side-lined me. It never has healed properly and I didn't play cricket again. In truth I didn't really make the effort to return. I never did fully take to league cricket. It wasn't so much fun. It seemed to me points were more important than pints.

Instead of drawing stumps at 7.30 and heading for the pub, games had to be completed. The statutory number of overs had to be bowled.

We batted first against Great Yarmouth at Southtown common. We rattled up a decent score. Chasing the runs, the home side soon fell well behind and were content to bat out their overs for a draw.

It got darker and darker and by quarter to nine it was almost impossible to follow the ball. Car headlights on the adjacent road were the only source of illumination. Deep in the outfield, I could hear ball hit bat but the only way I knew I had to field it was if the grass rustled somewhere near me.

When I finally got home that night I phoned my girlfriend – Miss H. She was wholly unconvinced we had been playing cricket after nightfall.

I did go back to friendly cricket for a while when staff at ECN formed Newsman Cricket Club. We played 20-over midweek games. It was a breath of fresh air after the intensity of leagues. Today, few will remember the game before leagues. To them it's always been about being top of the division.

In the winter I played for Carrow Hockey Club, also on the wonderful Lakenham Ground. I captained the side for a number of years. I was more confident playing hockey than cricket, and rarely missed a game.

We were a small club with only one team so it survived on loyalty, players being available almost every week. We did have some success but I recall one dreadful season. It was so bad we thought of renaming the club "Carrow Nil".

On one occasion I decided I was actually going to have a Saturday off. Mrs H could take the car to the hairdressers.

But the phone rang on Saturday morning. Someone had called off. Mrs H said she would get home as soon as she could. Bless her, she did and I roared off to Gorleston missing only a few minutes of the first half.

Mind you, there was a reason Mrs H was particularly co-operative on that occasion. It was just before Christmas and the young Brat Minor had his heart set on a particular toy; a glove puppet called Wrinkles. We tried everywhere but nowhere could we find Wrinkles for sale – except at Gorleston.

What a happy coincidence.

Hockey changed considerably with the introduction of artificial pitches. It was a different game. New skills had to be learned. The absence of bumps in the pitch meant close control of the ball was not only possible but essential. With the ball travelling so swiftly weighted diagonal passes to the wing were a thing of the past.

I adapted but missed the old-style of playing and didn't really regret it when I called it a day.

These all-weather pitches mean that games are rarely cancelled. Most have floodlights. Clubs can have all their teams at home on the same day, with the first game starting at 11am and the last at 5pm.

People think I'm crackers with my view on artificial surfaces. They can't understand why I'd rather play on a field where the grass was sometimes too long, there were bumps and divots so the ball didn't run true and, of course, in wet weather, if the game wasn't cancelled, we played in inches of mud.

But with leagues, time travelling to games increased and could take up most of Saturday. Something that probably didn't bother youngsters but for a family man with children, an understanding wife was needed. Thankfully Mrs H is such a wife. She'd see me depart in the morning to travel to somewhere such as Saffron Walden for a 2pm start, returning around 8pm having showered, had tea and a couple of pints – and no energy left to take her out.

Or, probably worse, setting off at lunchtime for a five o'clock start, not getting home until Match of the Day.

With my formative years largely spent clutching a cricket bat or hockey stick, what I needed is what every cricketer dreams of. A wife who will do the teas and sup a pint along with the rest of 'em.

When I met Mrs H I soon found out here was someone with whom I would never have an in-depth discussion about the LBW law.

And she didn't like beer.

But then they do say opposites attract. She was more than happy for me to disappear on a Saturday afternoon and play my games. And she uncomplainingly cleaned the grass stains of my whites and washed my hockey gear – providing I didn't leave it in the boot of the car until Friday.

She never insisted I miss a game so we could go to the sales. Something that saw some players subjected to utter disdain by their teammates when they reluctantly admitted that's why they weren't available the following week.

I lost count of the pairs of glasses smashed by hockey sticks, I've been to A&E a couple of times for minor repairs and, thanks to hockey and a divot on one of my beloved grass pitches, I have a knee joint that clicks when I stand up like a someone snapping a twig.

I spent a few days in hospital having my nose straightened following a mistimed hook and I have a crooked finger thanks to a misjudged catch.

I look back fondly on my sporting days. Fitness, camaraderie and a great exhaust valve following a difficult week at work.

And it meant Mrs H and I had our own space. I suspect on dreary Saturday afternoons in winter when I'm under her feet, there are times when she wishes I was still playing.

Norwich Mercury and Advertiser

1988 - 1990

This selection of columns from the Norwich Mercury and Advertiser illustrates that sport is so much more than just what happens on the field on a Saturday afternoon. The running of clubs, the impact on families and what happens when you get injured are among the many aspects to being involved with sport. Sport kept me fit, introduced me to people I would not otherwise have met and took me to places I didn't know existed.

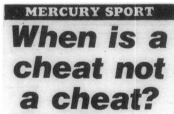

MERCURY SPORT

When is a cheat not a cheat?

By Neil Haverson

I WAS playing cards with my children last weekend.

We were playing a game of pairs — you know the one, where the cards are spread out face down and each player has a go at turning over two cards to see if he can get a matching pair.

The knack is to remember which cards have been turned over.

My son and I were desperately trying to store the information in our memories, neither of which is very good.

He cannot remember where he has put a particular toy two minutes after he has been playing with it. It has reached the stage where I climb the stairs to get something from the bedroom but by the time I arrive on the landing I have completely forgotten the purpose of my journey.

WINNING

My daughter, on the other hand, forgets nothing. This is most useful when you cannot find your car keys but most embarrassing when she ...

Indeed it was. She has reached the age where, by studying the blemishes on the cards, she can tell what they are when they are face down.

I wonder where you draw the line between cheating with premeditation and spontaneously taking advantage of an opportunity that suddenly presents itself.

For example, to mention him yet again, Maradonna did not go on ...

mount, Landing Officer he was racing on the track at Delta Downs, Louisiana, against eight rivals in thick fog.

When out of sight of the officials, he pulled his horse up and waited in the fog until the runners came round again. He rejoined the field and romped triumphantly home to a 24-length victory. He was subsequently disqualified and suspended for the rest of the season.

Warming to the idea, I had a dig around to see if I could find any other instances of deliberate cheating. Oddly enough most of the cases I came across were attempts to appear successful at the sport and not to win for financial gain. At least four examples relate to the Olympic games and were not, I should add, of the Ben Johnson variety.

In 1904 at the St Louis Olympics, marathon runner Fred Lorz hitched a lift on a truck when he got cramp after 10 miles. He won the race easily and was about to receive the gold medal from Alice Roosevelt when the real winner came running into the stadium and blew the ...

Fighting off the stomach bouncer

I was languishing in a piping hot bath. Eyes shut, I was dreaming contentedly. Michael Holding was steaming in off his long run. He arrived at the wicket and sent down a particularly quick one. Gracefully, I moved onto the front foot and effortlessly stroked the ball majestically through the covers. As it leapt over the ropes the capacity crowd stood in rapturous applause.

Suddenly I was brought back to earth as the bathroom door crashed open and my wife came in, "Good heavens," she exclaimed, "look at the size of that. I should think you're embarrassed in the changing room with that."

She was, as you will already have guessed, referring to the size of my stomach. It enjoyed some expansion over the festive period and, as yet, has not been persuaded to go back into shape. To be honest, I haven't tried that hard. Not until, that is, my fantasy test innings was so hurtfully bought to a close.

I babbled something about light being refracted through water causing an optical illusion, but, if you will pardon the expression, it didn't wash. I am now on rations.

Food and sport are not happy bedfellows. The right kind of food in the right quantities at the right time is ideal. Modern living does not always play ball with this. The only time that I am able to control with ease my diet is on the day of a match. This was made possible by an occasion some years back at a training session.

Only recently married, I sat down one evening after work and consumed a great feast prepared by my new wife. They do that sort of thing for you when you are just married. Suitably replete, I grabbed my gear and went for some pre-season training. It was a warm September evening and, after a couple of jogs round the perimeter of the field, I found myself slightly more short of breath than usual. There followed a few press-ups, sit-ups and sprints. By now I was beginning to feel quite queezy.

Anybody who has experienced this will know only too well what I mean. Your stomach feels as though you have drunk a pint of mercury. Your respiratory system refuses to function, you cannot breathe in or out. I remember lying on the ground, my mouth opening and closing like a demented goldfish. Someone remarked how precisely the colour of my face matched the grass.

I staggered to the dressing room and collapsed on the bench. As I lay there I became aware of a low moaning. There in the corner was our left back. His face contorted with pain, he just managed to raise his hand. I realised that he was trying to say something. Could it be a last message for his wife if the worst came to the worst?

I hastened to him as best I could and put my ear close to his mouth. He managed to utter just five words. "Fish fingers, chips and beans," he groaned. I could hardly tell his wife that. "Hello, Mary. Derek went quietly. He said to tell you…"

We lay there for around 15 minutes clutching our respective abdomens. The feeling that every organ between neck and waist had been shuffled gradually receded. We took no further part in that night's training other than to adjourn to the hostelry after a shower. Too ashamed to admit to our gluttony, our agreed story was that we must have picked up some virus.

Never again. The kids are now used to a light Saturday lunch following hard on the heels of their Weetabix. I am applying myself to this match-day dedication every day. I am also going to repair the lock on the bathroom door.

Norwich Mercury and Advertiser, Friday, July 29, 1988

Suffering for the sportsman's life

I thought that I might mention the sports widow this week. I thought I might, but then I wondered if I would be making life difficult for those with unsympathetic partners. What the heck, I concluded. Do our spouses know just what we go through for our sport?

First let me say that she who lets me out to play on Saturday afternoons has always been more than fair. She has moulded holidays around important matches, scheduled meals to meet departure times for long away games and acted as a telephone answering service when I have served on the committee.

Actually, I'm not sure if she has ever twigged that our wedding took place on the only blank date in the fixture list that year. That's not as bad as one chap I know. He opened his married life at 11.30am and the batting at 2.30pm.

However, I digress. Back to what we endure to partake of our sport. Believe you me girls, we realise that you've been working hard too. There you are, stuck with the kids all week and then what happens? We put in a brief appearance on a Saturday morning, then clear off to our game.

You seem to find it a trifle irritating but you must understand that we'd much rather be at home painting the bathroom or helping the children construct unrecognisable things out of Lego.

Instead we set off for a cricket match and just look at what we have to put up with. Our side are batting and we are put in at number seven. This means that we have to spend a couple of hours in the sun until we are needed. Stretched out, we lie there wondering how you are coping and worrying about when we can fit the decorating in.

Shortly before the tea interval we are called to the wicket to rattle up some quick runs. We stay there until the end of the innings, and by the time we have got our pads off, all the best sandwiches have gone and our cup of tea is cold.

When we take the field it's bound to start raining. Two hours fielding in a steady drizzle with the ball like a piece of soap. It's impossible to catch it and wherever we field so the airborne ball follows. At the end of the game we must have a shower. You wouldn't want us coming home all sweaty now, would you?

After the match it is essential that the game is fully analysed. For sheer convenience, and for no other reason, this discussion usually takes place in the pub. What choice do we have but to go along? We can't be left out. Someone buys us a drink and, as you know, a chap can't walk out without buying his round.

Now, I know we said that we would be home by 9 o'clock but they want to play darts and need one more to make up a four. We can't let the lads down.

Finally we arrive home exhausted and starving hungry, and what do we get? Tongue and cold shoulder. We've coped with all this and all you want to do is tell us how young Marmaduke kicked his football through the kitchen window. And why get so angry when we ask if it was with his left or right foot? He could be showing early promise.

Then you sever diplomatic relations completely just because we mention that there are a couple of knock-out cup games midweek.

It really is a hard life being a sportsman.

Sporting pull-up by the boot laces

I have just bought a new pair of laces for my boots. That may not seem a startling revelation, but it is when you consider this. The laces in my cricket boots have lasted two full seasons. As with my football boots they are often put away damp with the same result after five or six weeks.

As I am hastily tying them to get out on the field, they snap. The only thing to do is to tie a knot in them. After a few weeks they have been joined so many times that the knots prevent me pulling the laces tight.

I have been experiencing this difficulty with my football boots for about a season and a half. Contrary to any rumours emanating from the clubs for whom I play, my failure to renew them is not due to meanness. My problem is that for some things I have the memory retention capabilities of a sparrow.

As I yank off my boots after a game I promise myself that the first job on Monday will be to buy a new pair of laces. However, by the time the first mouthful of the post-match pint has made its journey to the stomach, such a detail has fled my memory.

She who lets me out to play on Saturday afternoons is unsympathetic and of no help. Her argument being that she does not expect me to remind her to get a new pair of tights when she needs them, so why should she help me look after my playthings?

Looking after kit differs in hockey to football. With hockey, while the club might provide the shirt, it is the custodian of the garment who is responsible for washing it. The problem here is that out of the team of 11, each wife or mother may use a combination of washing machine and soap powder. The result is that what started as a perfect line-up of identical colours soon ends up looking like a Dulux paint colour chart.

In football of course one person is responsible for laundering all the team's kit. A colleague who plays for a local club tells me that the difficulty here is the timing of the wash.

The shirt monitor for his team usually dashes to the laundrette on the morning of the game.

This means that the following week's team selection is limited to those players not suffering from pneumonia.

More personal apparel is of course down to the individual. I remember my first attempt at buying what is commonly known as a jock strap. I was around 16 at the time and was not sure whether the words "jock strap" should be said in public.

I was briefed (no pun intended) by my mother to ask for an athletic support. Armed with this phrase I marched into the sports shop. To my adolescent horror there was a woman serving. I decided to bide my time and wait for a male assistant.

To avoid suspicion I began to study intensely various pieces of sports equipment. No male person appeared. Meanwhile, I could be seen with a squash racket leaping around the store performing lightning back hands as if testing its weight. Then some flowing off drives as I pretended to sample a cricket bat.

Looking back on this, a parallel can be drawn with other shopping expeditions of the acne era. It's around this age that pimply teenagers pluck up courage to make their first birth control purchases. The difference between this and my case is that mine was due to need.

The acquisition of these other devices was merely to keep face with one's friends whose pockets always seemed to be full of the wretched things. Neither they nor you had the remotest chance of actually using one.

Back in the sports shop, I had finally arrived at the weight lifting gear. Rather than risk a hernia I decided that I had better ask the woman for what I wanted. I sucked in a deep breath and blurted out: "Could I have an athletic support please?"

"Pardon?" she replied.

"I need an athletic support," I repeated.

"Oh!" she exclaimed, "You want a jock strap."

Norwich Mercury and Advertiser, Friday, January 13, 1989

Early start could lead to a slip-up

In an unguarded moment last week, I let something slip that could have severely curtailed my weekend activities. I was about to leave for the match when she who lets me out to play on Saturday afternoons casually said: "You're leaving early today."

"We start at 2.15 you know," I replied. As I said it I knew that it was a mistake. She has never bothered with mere details such as specific starting times. What she thinks we do when it gets dark early I have no idea.

"If you start that early," she said with inspiration, "then you'll be home early." This was serious. Think on feet, Haverson. Talk your way out of this one. I decided to adopt the tactics used by Rene in "Allo Allo" when his wife catches him cuddling that rather attractive waitress.

"You stupid woman," I responded firmly. "Do you not know that we 'ave to 'ave a shower after ze game." Yes, I even threw in a bit of accent to make it sound convincing.

"Then we discuss ze game and then we talk over tactics for ze next match."

That really was asking for it. If she knew our team and tactics, she would know that the two do not normally appear in the same sentence.

I got away with it. "Oh," was her only reply. I'm surprised that she has not spotted the odd telltale sign. Like, if I have a shower after a game, how come my hair is always bone dry by the time I get home?

She has never queried how I manage to arrive back from an away match at, say Ipswich, the same time as I roll in from a home fixture. The truth is that the post-match pint figures prominently in home games but with away matches where driving is involved there is a tendency not to hang around.

After the match players tend to leave in dribs and drabs. There are usually one or two who dash off as soon as the final whistle has sounded. We had a chap who used to throw on a track suit and zoom out of the door clutching his shopping list to perform a quick circuit of Tesco.

Others drift away mumbling things like: "Going out to dinner. Don't want to go but better show willing." Finally, all that's left is the hard core of drinkers. This usually consists of those who are single, those about to become single and that one member in every club who has got it sussed and comes and goes when he pleases.

If you are a bit late there are always one or two handy excuses. Norwich were at home, I had to wait for the football traffic to clear. Or, a player got injured and I had to run him up to casualty. As a last resort, try this. Stop the car a short distance from home, dive under the bonnet and cover your hands with grease. When you get home, simply walk in the door, display your oily fingers and make a supporting comment such as: "We must get that dammed carburettor fixed."

Now that I have given you all those helpful tips, do me a favour. When you've read this week's paper, put it under the dog bowl or something. For goodness sake don't let my wife see it.

The one time my kids co-operated

*"*I know the British Open is a very big deal but there are more important things in life. The most important is my family." So said golfer Mark Calcavecchia following his victory at Royal Troon.

He was referring to the fact that his wife, Sheryl, was about to give birth to their first child. Had she gone into labour before the last round, he says that he would have left for home immediately.

I am sure that he is grateful that he did not have to make that decision. What an agonising situation he would have been in. While you don't get many chances for a crack at The Open, the times when you can be at the birth of your child are equally few and far between.

I have no doubt that he would have flown home and I think that he would have been, in my opinion, quite right too. I, along with many other people, was horrified when, during the last football season, Martin Allen of Queens Park Rangers was fined by manager Trevor Francis for attending the birth of his first child.

Allen had travelled to Newcastle but returned to London when his wife went into labour. Francis said that footballers were paid a lot of money and that their club should come first. He later admitted that he had his wife induced for the birth of their child to suit his footballing commitments.

That was Francis' decision but in Allen's case, suppose something had gone wrong at the birth. It would be Allen and not Francis that would have to live with that guilt. It was refreshing to hear Calcavecchia put big money and ambition in second place to his wife.

The arrival of my two is about the only incident of co-operation that I have received from the little horrors since they made their presence felt on this planet. Both were born on a Monday. This fitted in nicely with weekend sport.

Having completed the previous Saturday fixture without incident the timely early week births meant that I was available for the delivery, on hand to see the first few days of parenthood through, then slip away for a few hours' break the following Saturday afternoon.

As I marched out clutching my hockey stick, the midwife gave me a withering look as she entered with her blood pressure kit.

I must admit that on the first-born it was a bit touch and go. The Saturday prior to the Monday when she finally put in an appearance involved an away fixture at Ely. I travelled separately to the rest of the team so that I could return home immediately after the game.

I left at the last minute, telephoning on arrival at Ely. After the match I called again to make sure that nothing had happened. My wife asked if we had won. It's a good job that we had lost. I am sure that the shock of hearing that we actually scored a victory would have immediately sent her into labour.

All through the game I wondered if there was a police car touring Ely broadcasting an appeal for me: "Here is a message for Neil Haverson, she who lets you out to play on Saturday afternoons is now having contractions every seven minutes."

After the event I proudly telephoned my mates to tell them the news. They had their priorities right as usual. Before any word of congratulations was offered there was the instant reaction: "You'll be alright for Saturday won't you?"

Norwich Mercury and Advertiser, Thursday, December 21, 1989

Fresh kit for Christmas please, Santa

Mr S Claus,
The North Pole.

Dear Santa,

I hope this letter reaches you in time. I don't think you can have received the one I sent last year. Or perhaps I did not make myself clear. When I said that I would like a pair of Gary Lineker football boots, I meant a pair that I can wear, not the ones that dangle from the interior mirror of the car.

Thank you for including the video of the highlights of Tranmere Rovers' 1953-54 season. I haven't actually watched it yet but I'm sure it will be worth waiting for.

I do hope that it's not too late to slap in a request to be added to the chimney list for this year. I would have written earlier, but she who lets me out to play on Saturday afternoons has only just pointed out a few problems on the kit front, so I thought that you might be able to help with a few replacements.

You know how, with a car, everything seems to go at once. Just as you notice that the tyres need replacing so the battery dies on you. Then the alternator packs up. All this happens at MOT time and you are subjected to the mechanic with the woefully shaking head who tells you in multiples of £20 what needs doing to your car to pass the test.

This probably happens to you with your sleigh. No doubt, all the reindeer get clapped out at once. Well, the same is true of my gear. The good lady was ironing my hockey shirt the other evening when she discovered that the fabric was rather like our forward line, a bit thin in places. Next came the hurtful remark.

"If you really are intending to carry on playing next season," she said pointedly, "you will have to have a new shirt." Quite what she meant by this I'm not sure. I do not recall mentioning that retirement is imminent. Perhaps some of my team-mates have had a word with her in an attempt to ease me gently towards the touch-line.

Next she held my shorts, demonstrating the elastic was a bit like our defence, somewhat overstretched.

The only explanation that we can come up with for not having noticed this is that as the elastic has slackened, so my stomach has expanded, thereby retaining my shorts at a respectable level.

All this prompted a close inspection of the remainder of the kit. Holes were found in my socks. The reason for their disintegration was subsequently traced to a split in each of my boots.

If you had got it right last year I would have been saved a pair of socks. If you can find the necessary in your sack this year, I will be saved a substantial investment.

Bearing in mind your mix-up over my football boots, please note that my son's request for a Porsche refers to the Matchbox series, not the real thing. In view of this, please cancel my daughter's request for a set of wheel clamps.

Yours in anticipation,

Neil Haverson

PS If the children leave out one of my wife's rock cakes for you, I can accept no responsibility if you actually eat it.

When is a cheat not a cheat?

I was playing cards with my children last weekend. We were playing a game of pairs - you know the one, where the cards are spread out face down and each player has a go at turning over two cards to see if he can get a matching pair.

The knack is to remember which cards have been turned over.

My son and I were desperately trying to store the information in our memories, neither of which is very good.

He cannot remember where he has put a particular toy two minutes after he has been playing with it. It has reached the stage where I climb the stairs to get something from the bedroom, but by the time I arrive on the landing I have completely forgotten the purpose of my journey.

My daughter, on the other hand, forgets nothing. This is most useful when you cannot find your car keys but most embarrassing when she tells the neighbour what you said, some months previously, about the shape of his wife.

Back to the card game. This young female maverick was, of course, winning. However, she was steaming to such an emphatic victory that it just had to be due to more than the quality of her memory.

Indeed it was. She has reached the age where, by studying the blemishes on the cards, she can tell what they are when they are face down.

I wonder where you draw the line between cheating with premeditation and spontaneously taking advantage of an opportunity that suddenly presents itself.

For example, Argentine footballer Diego Maradona did not go on the field in his side's World Cup game against England in 1986 with the decided intent of handling the ball into the net. He just "grabbed" the opportunity when it came.

This idle thought crossed my mind when, humiliated at cards, I turned to the paper and spotted a story about American jockey Sylvester Carmouche. On his mount, Landing Officer, he was racing on the track at Delta Down, Louisiana, against eight rivals in thick fog.

When out of sight of the officials, he pulled his horse up and waited in the fog until the runners came around again. He rejoined the field and romped triumphantly home to a 24-length victory. He was subsequently disqualified and suspended for the rest of the season.

Warming to the idea, I had a dig around to see if I could find any other instances of deliberate cheating. Oddly enough, most of the cases I came across were attempts to appear successful at the sport and not to win for financial gain. At least four examples relate to the Olympic Games and were not, I should add, of the Ben Johnson* variety.

In 1904 at the St Louis Olympics, marathon runner Fred Lorz hitched a lift on a truck when he got cramp after 10 miles. He won the race easily and was about to receive the gold medal from Alice Roosevelt when the real winner came running into the stadium and blew the gaff.

I remember the incident in the 1976 Montréal Olympics when the Russian pentathlete rigged his epee with an electrical circuit which registered non-existent hits.

After his disqualification he was escorted back to the USSR by two KGB guards. I wonder what happened to him. He's probably a senior member of the Politburo now.

When South Africa were involved in international cricket, Australia's Ian Chappell was given out in a Johannesburg Test match, caught by home player Tiger Lance. Chappell queried with Lance whether he had actually caught the ball. Lance confirmed that he had and Chappell walked.

After close of play Chappell again asked if it was a clean catch. Lance replied: "You never asked me if it bounced first."

There are several other instances which make the odd handball look quite fair. However, you might do well to pay close attention next time there is a particularly foggy day at Sloughbottom.

If the opposition are awarded a spot-kick, make sure that the person who takes the penalty was on the field at the start and didn't sneak on through the mist.

In fact, it's probably worth counting how many players your opponents have on the field in the first place…

*Canadian sprinter Ben Johnson was stripped of his 1988 Olympic medals for doping offences.

Norwich Mercury and Advertiser, Friday, April 6, 1990

Well turned out for kit inspection

" It was a terrible game today, I played really badly." "Did you dear, I am sorry. Do you know what those two so-and-sos did to the cat this afternoon with a reel of Sellotape…?"

I know that you girls do take an interest in our sport and that type of reaction which sometimes come from you know who is not absolutely fair. I have told she who lets me out to play on Saturday afternoons of the odd sporting achievement and actually heard her repeating it to somebody, so I know that she does take it all in.

"Oh, he is in a good mood this morning. He had a hard game yesterday but was able to get out of bed without assistance this morning."

In fact I have found an area where the ladies do get a bit concerned. No, it's not about our ability to turn on a sixpence and fire home an unstoppable shot or the ease with which we are able to play a backhand lob. It is our appearance. We need not be the best hookers of a short pitched ball, but we must look well turned-out.

I wrote before Christmas of the open-plan boots I had been playing in. Well, I am ashamed to say that I have only just disposed of them in favour of something more sophisticated. My excuse is, of course, high interest rates and the advent of the poll tax.

However, the other day, my wife caught me inspecting the size of one of the splits. I was only checking that it was not actually bigger than my foot.

"You're not still wearing those are you?" she asked in amazement. I mumbled something about it having been a dry winter so it had not been too uncomfortable and anyway, think of the money I had saved.

"Whatever must they think of me in the dressing room when you produce those moth-eaten old things?" she exploded. Hang on a minute. What must they think of HER because MY boots are split? I should have let the matter rest there, but no. I had to ask the reason for her reputation being at stake over my boots.

"They'll think that I am not bothered about you. It's the same with your shirt." What? My shirt? What has that got to do with anything?

"Don't tell me my shirt is coming apart as well." Even as I spoke, I realised what was coming. I am notoriously bad at putting out my kit for the wash. It's all that I can do to lug it indoors on a Saturday after a tough game, let alone extract it from the bag.

I usually remember around Thursday that it needs de-caking of mud and tentatively submit it for scrubbing. This means that it is getting near departure time for the next week's game by the time that the biological powder has done its best and the wretched stuff is dry.

"Don't bother to iron it," I pipe up helpfully as the shirt is hurled unceremoniously on to the ironing board and attacked with a spray of steam.

Off she goes again. "I'm not letting you play in a creased shirt. Whatever will they think of me?" Why, I hear you cry, do I not iron it myself? I don't see the point in ironing it at all.

Surely it cannot be worth ironing the shirt when it is only destined to play host to a sweaty body that in all probability will, at some stage, make contact with other perspiring persons and a certain amount of mud.

This is not the point, it is those vital seconds in the changing room when the shirt is produced from the kit bag. There must be some clandestine ritual of pre-match kit inspection that I have not noticed.

I am not complaining and I do appreciate that she looks out for me in this way. And yes, I do feel guilty that I don't make sure that my kit is out for a wash straight after the game. We have all changed next to the person who could do with a good laundering himself, let alone his gear. However, next time I inspect my boots it will be in private.

Norwich Mercury and Advertiser, Friday, June 15, 1990

The day the womenfolk kicked sand in our faces

What is all this fuss about some football competition taking place in Italy?* In my book the main event on the soccer calendar took place a couple of weeks ago on Hemsby beach.

Admittedly, there was no publicity given to the occasion. The low-key approach was not attributable to a desire to avoid potential crowd trouble, so much as the fact that the exact stretch of sand where the encounter was to take place was only selected at the last minute.

The match was between the male half of the Haversons - me and our five-year-old son - and the female half, consisting of she who lets me out to play on Saturday afternoons and our seven-year-old daughter.

I must say at this point that I now have a jaundiced view of female sportsmanship, not to mention some highly debatable tactics. And why do they have to shriek so much?

All right yes, we males lost, but my comments are not due to sour grapes… well perhaps just a bit. But let me set the facts before you and you may judge for yourself.

In the end the event was staged over two days. This was not the original plan - but a whinging female tactic caused the game to be abandoned at half-time.

It was a fairly even half after the females had assured themselves that the goalposts, constructed out of piles of sand, were in line.

This delay unsettled us and led to suggestions that Haversons of the male gender do not possess the big match temperament.

Anyway the girls, mainly through large slices of luck, were leading 3-2 when the game was suddenly halted.

We were just coming back strongly and pressing for the equaliser when my wife announced that it was half-time. This was followed immediately by a statement that the match would have to be abandoned as she had broken the nail on the big toe of her goal-scoring foot.

What? This just happened to be a ruse because they were beginning to crack under our skilful use of the sloping sands. Can you imagine England striker Peter Beardsley calling for a game to be postponed because he had a fractured bootlace?

However, we sporting males gallantly agreed to the postponement and a rematch was arranged for the following day at low water.

As the tide had washed away the previous day's pitch a new stadium was swiftly dug. But things got off on the wrong foot as soon as we lined up for the kick-off.

The public address system - in the form of my daughter - announced that the previous day's encounter was considered as a victory for the ladies and that the current game was merely an opportunity for us males to redress the balance.

We immediately lodged an official protest. While we were doing this it appeared that the game had started and we found ourselves 1-0 down. We abandoned our appeal and launched into the attack.

The game was fast and furious, with a liberal sprinkling of hysterical female screaming as goals went in at either end. The score crept up to 5-5.

We males were suffering badly for attempting to stick to the rules. When threatened with being robbed of the ball, daughter realised that when she was persuaded to put it down again she had manoeuvred herself into an excellent scoring position.

Things degenerated as the same girl became adept at "handing off" her brother when they went for a 50-50 ball. With the score at 6-6 I found myself exposed.

My team-mate was lying prostrate on the half-way line spitting furiously, claiming that his sister had kicked sand in his face when he had the ball at his feet in front of an open goal.

So there I was, facing alone two females hungry for victory. As there were no witnesses I decided that I would break the habits of a lifetime and fling myself at my wife's feet.

I missed, she didn't. As the ball cross the line those wretched females announced that it was the end of the game and promptly walked off the pitch.

There you have it. Is this not a sporting travesty? Highlights of this match unfortunately will not be available on video, so you must make up your own minds from my quite unbiased account.

Rest assured, we will have our revenge. On a beach somewhere in Norfolk a rematch will be staged before the summer is through.

*The football World Cup was staged in Italy in 1990.

Syrup of figs helps batsmen get the runs

I spotted that the International Cricket Council is looking at the possibility of more sponsorship for the sport. To provide an independent panel of umpires will cost, it is estimated, somewhere in the region of half-a-million pounds a season - so additional finance is essential and sponsorship is seen as the answer.

Sponsors, of course, want exposure. So one possibility being considered is advertising on the back of the umpires' white coats.

I say chaps, this just isn't cricket! The sport is being taken over by commercialism!

But then again, I suppose things have to be paid for.

To give the sponsors value for money, no doubt we shall be in for lots of close-up shots of the umpire – "Let's see again from behind the umpire how Dickie Bird signals that four."

Umpires will probably demand appearance money - and who wouldn't if you were to place yourself in front of millions of viewers with something like, "Today's game is brought to you by Doggybix" plastered on your back?

Perhaps it need not be just the game that is sponsored. Individual elements could attract advertisers. A slogan on the umpire's sleeve announcing: "Umpires' signals brought to you in association with John Brown's Bitter. It's what your right arm's for."

How about the scores? "Scores sponsored by syrup of figs. Give your team syrup of figs and make sure the batsmen get the runs."

Maybe those announcements over the Tannoy when they give out such information as bowling figures will be accompanied by advertising jingles. "Eddie Hemmings 15 overs, two maidens, 3-85. Eddie's sweater comes from Man at War on Want."

The sponsors of the Nat West trophy already have their names chalked on the sacred turf right under the camera lens. This all seems a bit Americanised to me.

I wonder how long it will be before we see Mike Gatting* making his entrance on to the field to the accompaniment of singing, dancing cheer leaders.

*Mike Gatting was England cricket captain from 1986-88.

Hooking with a hangover: Batting after a heavy night versus the Romford Recorder on the LN&A tour in 1968.

Still single: Quentin and I pose outside St Cuthbert's Church, Thetford as we await the arrival of Miss H.
Picture: Paul Hewitt.

Pipe dreams: I became an aspiring model for this picture taken in the late 1960s for a Lynn News & Advertiser promotional advertisement. Picture courtesy Lynn News.

They bought it in the estate agent's office....

....but they saw it in the Eastern Daily Press

Shades of grey: On February 16, 1971 ECN trialled its first process colour printing with an advertisement in the EDP. I played the part of a husband with receptionist Christine Morley playing my wife. Mike Tubby from management accounts was the estate agent. I'm wearing brown Hush Puppies, but they printed as grey.

Male order: Looking like something out of a catalogue I posed again in 2008 on Mousehold Heath in Norwich for a feature on outdoor clothing.
Picture: Antony Kelly, Archant.

So long to the flong: One of the last flongs to be used for platemaking at ECN. This one was for page 7 of the Eastern Evening News of September 15, 1971.
Picture Paul Hewitt

All set: The LN&A cricket team about to board the bus for the 1966 tour. Left to right: Peter Jowitt (Pedge), Pete Jenkins, Brian Kimber, the driver, Lawry Hunter, Craig Seaton, me, Neil Wiseman, Bev Bargewell, John (Sam) Hardy, Mick Sands, John Allen, John Gathercole. Picture courtesy Lynn News.

Planning: A meeting in October, 1989 when I was Admin Manager, discussing newspaper page plans. Left to right: Me, John Gardner, Jane Holbrook, Linda Bullent, Wendy Jones.
Picture: Archant

Lines of type: Invented in 1886, the linotype machine transformed typesetting enabling a small number of operators to set type for a large number of pages.
Picture Archant.

Ruth Watson: To the country house rescue in East Anglia

Let's Talk

Issue 103 April 2011
ONLY £1.50

WIN: A three-night break in Jersey

ROGER LLOYD PACK
Norfolk's light skies

WIN: Sunblinds worth £250

- Suffolk cyclist's ride for charity
- Adrian Bell's East Anglian legacy
- Norfolk woman's HGV challenge

Memory Lane: ten pages of great pictures from the past

FREE for every reader: Pure Piano CD; sensational Magnolia Yellow River

Lucky break: A chance encounter led to my interview with the late actor Roger Lloyd Pack, star of Only Fools and Horses and The Vicar of Dibley. It turned out to be a best-selling issue for Let's Talk.

Bundled up: Packing the newspapers ready for dispatch at ECN's Redwell Street premises which they occupied until 1969.
Picture Archant

Battle ground: I returned to my old primary school at Downham Market in 2009 for a schooldays feature. Aged around nine I had a fight under this tree, which I was actually winning until a teacher stepped in. Picture: Matthew Usher, Archant

On air: With Nick Conrad at West Somerton recording the feature on the Norfolk Giant for Radio Norfolk. Picture: Mrs H.

Hot off the press: One of the first editions of the Evening News to be printed in 1995 at Archant's newly built print centre on Broadland Business Park, Norwich. Picture: Archant.

Top of the pops: With Keith Skues in the Radio Norfolk studio on the night we played the Let's Talk readers' top twenty.

How do you do it? Gerry Marsden told Roy Strowger and me exactly how before he went on stage at Great Yarmouth in 2003.

Loud and clear, the Brats are in action

I must start this week with an apology. Well, two actually, both relating to incidents in the city last Saturday.

Firstly, if you were in the All Saints Green area around lunchtime, I am sorry if you were denied the conclusion of a rather loud pronouncement by Brat Major as her mother hastily cut short her comments in mid sentence.

"If that lady's skirt was any shorter . . ." as she exclaimed her observation Mrs H grabbed her shoulder and neither the lady herself nor other passers-by knew what was in the young fashion expert's mind.

The second apology is offered to those enjoying a snack in the restaurant of a well-known department store. Fortunately, I was not there at this point but Mrs H has given me all the embarrassing details.

You will know which store I mean when I tell you it's the one where pigeons sit outside the windows. You will also recall the children when I tell you that one, the girl, was consuming a doughnut like it was her last meal and the boy was attempting to eat a cream cake of which most of the cream was transferred from the cake to his left sleeve. Suddenly they espied two pigeons through the window.

"Mum, why has one pigeon got its beak inside the others?" Mrs H, intent on buttering a scone, suggested that one must be a young bird and was being fed. There was a short pause before those at surrounding tables had their attention drawn to renewed activity outside the window.

"Look what they're doing now? What are they doing, mum?" cried two excited voices in unison. Choking on her scone Mrs H hissed through her active teeth for them to keep their voices down.

"They're making love," she growled. The wiser Brat Major flushed slightly. Her brother, since the explanation had nothing to do with football, resumed his task of redistributing the cream from his cake to as much of his clothing as possible.

Perhaps it's the time of year that made these young pigeons' thoughts turn to billing and cooing. It certainly affects us. Spring heralds the arrival of the washing opinion at Fortress Haverson and this alone caused last week's shopping trip to be delayed.

Throughout the winter, when the weather is damp, cold and horrible and we need the heating on, the radiators are smothered with clothes that are either drying or airing. Mrs H also has a clothes horse which she stands in the bath. Not only do you have to heave it out when you want a bath but also stagger round with wet knickers slapping you in the face while you find somewhere to stand it.

Worse still is that, by spring, all the condensation caused by the damp breeds a healthy growth of mould. I have just harvested last year's crop when I decorated the bathroom.

Mrs H sets out to take full advantage of the "good dry" the milder windy conditions bring. This is fine except for one thing, which we experienced last Saturday before we embarked on our outing.

As usual, Mrs H was running late. Even the Brats were ready. Madame had finally agreed with her mother a mutually acceptable outfit. The young chancellor had counted his money several times and, whilst arriving at a different total on each occasion, had allocated himself sufficient funds to squander on some tape by an obscure pop group.

Both had even been persuaded to go to the toilet. Why do children fight against this so much before going out as if it is a matter of principle? The times we have got a few miles up the road and that pathetic little voice pipes up that they "just can't wait."

Anyway, there we were booted and spurred. The sound of Mrs H coming downstairs gave us hope of an imminent departure. Alas, when she hove into view, it was not her handbag that she was carrying but a basket of washing and a bag of clothes pegs.

"Must just peg these out. There's a good dry today." Before we could protest, she pushed past with the comment "Your jeans will only smell if I don't hang them out in the fresh air."

There are times when I would rather be a pigeon.

Eastern Daily Press

1990-

The Fortress H dispatches are simply everyday stories of family folk. When I started writing them I had no idea they would still be gracing the pages of the Eastern Daily Press some 27 years later. But family life evolves, it is ever-changing, as does my byline picture! This selection of columns, first published between 1990 and 2016 shows how my family has continually provided me with material.

Neil Haverson

IN MY VIEW

The art of the male apology

She was sitting on a low wall looking decidedly at odds with the world. He was standing at right angles to her shuffling uncomfortably from foot to foot. Clearly all was not hearts and flowers between them. As I walked past she said just one sentence that painted practically the entire picture for me.

"Not until you say it meaningfully," she said, oblivious to the rest of the world.

All was now clear. He had committed a misdemeanour and was subsequently suffering from insincere apology syndrome. I had no idea what the offence was but somehow my sympathy went out to him. I have been there and so, I am sure, have most of the male population.

He may have made a passing reference to the texture of her fruit cakes or touched briefly on the close resemblance that she has to her mother. It may even have been that he did not know what he had done and was merely trying to apologise for the sake of a quiet life. I have definitely been there!

At the risk of appearing nosy, I could not resist glancing over my shoulder after I had gone a hundred yards or so up the road. She was striding off in a northerly direction and he was shambling uncomfortably behind.

Round one was over. Round two would probably take place in the car, with the contest reaching its conclusion at home after a third round of indeterminate length.

So how do you apologise "meaningfully". Most of us have, I am sure, gone through the range. It starts with soft approach. Fling the arms wide, lay the head gently on one side and say: "Look, I'm sorry." Do not add at this stage: "I don't know what I have done, but I am sorry." This will only inflame the situation when you may just get away with it at the first attempt.

Avoid the white knuckle apology. This is a desperate expression of regret delivered with clenched fists and such passion that it is clear that sincerity does not figure in your strategy.

Don't set any precedents. Once you have done something tangible to make good the situation, it will be expected every time. For example, avoid offers of compensation. "I am so sorry. Look, I'll tell you what, to make it up to you I'll re-point the chimney at the weekend."

Also to be avoided is expenditure. This comes after the event when you turn up suitably contrite, clutching a bunch of withering carnations that have spent the day grappling with petrol fumes on the local garage forecourt until you spotted them, wilting, on your way home.

Rarely will a woman actually accept the apology. If you do strike optimum apology level, the best that you can hope for is a short silence. Don't get over-eager here and dive in with a change of subject. This may indicate that the point of contention is not important to you. "I am truly sorry... I see the cat has dug up those bedding plants you put in."

If you are not in the clear by now, I can offer no further advice. At this stage, whatever caused the argument has been lost in the verbal interchange.

Other things which bear no relation to the original point have been brought into play. You have been told that you drink too much and that your driving leaves a lot to be desired. You have countered with references to the time it takes her to get ready to go out and does she have to bite her nails while she is watching Coronation Street?

And so it goes on until a diversion dilutes the situation. This is usually the children putting their heads around the door saying: "Why are you two arguing? You tell us off when we do that."

By the way, I do hope that I have not offended any of you ladies with my comments. If I have, I am awfully sorry. No, really, I mean it.

Eastern Daily Press, Saturday, March 2, 1991

Please Miss, can I be foetal monitor?

It was an office that I do not usually have cause to enter in the course of my normal work, so I was unfamiliar with the layout. I walked in slightly hesitantly.

All was quiet with half-a-dozen people, heads down, hard at work. I spoke briefly to the person I had come to see and then, still slightly self-conscious, turned on my heel. I pulled open the door and swept out of the room. Straight into the darkness of a small cupboard.

I can assure you that there is nothing you can say or do to minimise the embarrassment in such circumstances. I emerged from the gloom to be confronted by six quizzical faces. I babbled something about how on earth did they work in such heat, selected another door, checked carefully that led to the outside world, and ran. I have not returned to that office since and keep my eyes dipped if I meet any of the incumbents in the corridor.

Nerves and stress make us do and say things that we would not normally contemplate. I remember when Brat Major was being born. I was there at the birth and Mrs H was lying on the bed with the action well under way. The sister suddenly said: "Now, where is the foetal monitor?"

Inspired by nerves, I replied in a voice that had a hint of hysteria in it: "Please, Miss, can I be foetal monitor today?" The subsequent withering look was so powerful that it was almost enough to cancel the plans for the conception of Brat Minor.

Later during her labour, Mrs H unwittingly saved me from further embarrassment through a similar stupid remark. Every time she had a painful contraction she had developed the habit of grabbing hold of my jumper and pulling hard. This caused me to assume suddenly a variety of ungainly positions.

Brat Major was showing a marked reluctance to join her anxious parents in the big world. So the midwife rolled up her sleeves to offer some encouragement. Like Nureyev lecturing a bunch of ballet students, she announced in haughty tones: "I am about to perform an episiotomy." This begged a reply and in a split-second several alternatives presented themselves in my brain for consideration. The thought of the sister springing athletically around the delivery room with an assortment of complicated movements was too much. Fortunately, nature intervened and I did not have time to put my foot in it.

As I engaged brain and opened my mouth, Mrs H had another contraction. She grabbed my jumper and yanked hard. I hurtled across the bed and landed on top of her like a wrestler going for a submission. My face ended up adjacent to the gas and air mask. Assisted by a couple of lungfuls of this I regained my equilibrium, by which time the sister was poised for action and my opportunity to be silly had passed.

Brat Major finally put in an appearance. While Mrs H was recovering I was sent to the fathers' room. Already, a grinning, self-satisfied, new father was in there. Unlike me, he was perfectly relaxed. He was using the telephone to inform his relatives of what, clearly to him, had been a single-handed triumph. "The cord was wrapped a couple of times round his neck. Soon sorted that out though," he said, as if he had been on hand with his penknife to save the day.

Then in I walked. A sweating, harassed individual clothed in an extremely baggy jumper and looking as though I had just gone five rounds with wrestler Giant Haystacks.

Eastern Daily Press, Saturday, April 18, 1992

Clutter, but no chaos, for Mrs H

In the Fortress motorpool is a small, ageing set of wheels. This is driven mainly by Mrs H. She uses it for Brat-ferrying, weekly raids on the supermarket and her spot of wheeler-dealing which helps to boost the Fortress coffers. It can often be seen after the early morning school run parked outside any one of a number of houses in the village.

I know this because when I get home from work, she lets slip that she met the female resident of one of the aforementioned number of houses at the school gates.

"She said 'Why don't you come and have a cup of coffee?' Well, I hadn't seen her for ages so I said that I'd go, just for a quick one. And guess what? You know that woman…" there then follows an update on the village gossip involving people of whom I have never heard who have done things that I would not dare.

The car gets Mrs H from A to B. How it manages to do this she does not want to know. She merely reports to me anything that she feels is faulty for me to get it fixed. It is not that which bothers me. The outside of the machine is kept clean by me, but the state of the inside is entirely down to Mrs H.

If it was the Brats' bedrooms or the tiny corner of the Fortress master bedroom which is allotted to me, she would go berserk. We are not allowed to let the mess build up, but take a glance in the car and see what it is like.

The full scale of the clutter was referred to me courtesy of a marmalade cat. I was driving the car one Saturday morning when this brave feline challenged me to deduct one of its lives, by scurrying across the road in front of me. He survived, but as I drew to a rapid halt I realised that the contents of the vehicle had rearranged themselves.

As the brakes took effect, a container of baby wipes and a can of de-icer emerged from under the passenger seat like a couple of acrobats entering stage left. They tumbled merrily into the foot well and continued to jockey position with each other for the rest of the journey.

I decided to check the rest of the interior. The small tunnel tray was bulging with artefacts. There was another can of de-icer, something to wipe mist off the windscreen, more baby wipes and several discarded car park tickets. Any spare space had a tissue rammed into it.

I groped under the driver's seat. Surely there could not be anything under there. Oh yes there was. Like a magician pulling rabbits out of a hat, I produced a shoe. And then another and another. Finally I had two pairs of shoes in my hands. That means, assuming that she has on a pair of shoes when she gets into the car, she has a choice of three pairs altogether.

Perhaps all women are like this. Now you know why they are slow to move away when the traffic lights turn to green. They are otherwise engaged in selecting a change of footwear.

The clobber on the back seat was easily identifiable as Brats' property. Bits of aeroplane and an assorted collection of Brat Major's hair accessories. The glove compartment was crammed full of things, from maps to sticking plasters. I decided to save the boot for another day.

The other week the car needed some work doing to it. Like everything else practical, my skills go little beyond topping up the radiator, so we had to call in Spannerman. He fixed the headlights which had decided to stick on main beam and put the wink back into the indicators, the absence of which had seen Mrs H resort to hand signals. I bet that caused confusion in the village. Was she turning right or acknowledging an invitation for coffee?

Spannerman also fitted a new choke cable. He told me later that he had accidentally left the old one under the seat. I mentioned this to Mrs H and, to my amazement, she knew it was there. So, in spite of the chaos, she does know where everything is in the car.

Oh, except one thing, that is. She has yet to discover that small hole about three inches in diameter fitted into the rear wing. You know the one I mean. Where the petrol goes in.

I'm being traded in for a new model

I arrived home last Friday night to be told that the Fortress Laundry service had been suspended. The program knob on the washing machine was faulty and, if left to its own devices, the appliance whirred away as if it were on a sponsored spin.

Mrs H had already reached for the service contract: "We'll be out within 48 hours." Fine, until you check the small-print. If the breakdown occurs on a Friday, you have to wait until after the weekend.

Anybody who has young children will know that to have the washing machine out of action is a disaster. Children can get a mark on a clean outfit without even getting it out of the drawer.

For example, Brat Minor is incapable of eating chocolate in the accepted manner. It spreads all around his mouth as if he is trying to absorb it through his face by some kind of osmosis. In spite of constant correction from his mother, he winds up his feeding session by wiping his mouth on his sleeve and rubbing his hands down his trousers.

This is just one instance. Throw in Brat Major with a couple of leaking pens and her refusal ever to wear slippers, preferring to pad around the house in white socks, and the loss of the laundry facility is desperate.

Telephone calls were made to sympathetic parties, and by Sunday great piles of clean washing were stacked around the place, courtesy of friends and relations. This presented Mrs H with a huge pile of ironing.

"Why does this sort of thing always happen to me?" she moaned as she set up the ironing board. "I look after the wretched thing when it lets me down."

She snatched one of my shirts, flung it onto the ironing board and began to vent her wrath on it with a steaming iron. Suddenly there was a sound like Brat Minor firing his cap-gun and a peculiar burning smell. The iron had taken the hump and come out in sympathy with the washing machine. As the iron ceased to steam, so Mrs H began.

"I told you there was something wrong with this iron." Yes, I had to be responsible in some way. "You'll have to take it back tomorrow." Another phone call and Mrs H's father arrived to donate his iron to the Fortress cause.

These appliances should be grateful that they are inanimate objects and impervious to the hurtful comments. If I am indisposed, my loss from the

Fortress work rota is such an inconvenience to Mrs H. Now, suppose she could ring up and have me fixed in the same way?

"Hello, is that Husband Maintenance? He's gone kaput again. Flat out on his back - claims he can't move a muscle."

"No problem, madam. We'll have somebody round in the morning. Sounds like his lethargy prevention programme has failed. We'll pop in a new circuit-board. Don't you worry, we'll soon have him washing up again."

"I would be grateful if you could. You know how it is being a housewife when the husband conks out. I've already had to borrow next-door's to eject a spider."

"Ah, I see from our records you have got one of the older models. They are susceptible to this problem when they have been in service as long as yours. Have you considered getting a new one? I am sure you could find somebody to take your old one off your hands."

You had better keep an eye on the classifieds. You might see me offered for sale. "New model thankfully allows disposal of worn husband. Not bad for age but some slack muscles. Not a handyman but tries hard.

"Washing-up reliable, has own Marigolds. Remembers birthdays but don't expect flowers. Can be seen working any evening between 6pm and midnight or any time at weekends. Any offer considered."

There, who could resist the last puppy in the shop? I'd better pack my suitcase - and my Marigolds.

Eastern Daily Press, Saturday, February 20, 1993

Running repairs pose a problem

The Fortress laundry service has been restored, with the washing machine back in working order. Now there is a blockage in the sewing department.

I remember this happened many years ago when we were first married. It was the lining of the mac, as I recall. When the repaired garment failed to materialise, being a brave new husband, I sent Mrs H a tongue-in-cheek memo requesting that my mac be given some priority as it was the rainy season.

There followed what was to become a familiar lecture on the hapless lot of the modern housewife, but the repair was done.

There was a minor blip recently. I began to thank Mrs H for buying me a new shirt. Then I realised that the shirt looked vaguely familiar. It transpired that it was one that had been submitted some months before to have a button sewn on and I had forgotten all about it. She claimed the delay was due to the fact that she had lost the button.

Before I am accused of being a typical useless male, yes, I can sew a button on. They don't stay on for long, but I can do it. Anyway, every time I offer, Mrs H insists on doing it. This is because she thinks it is her job as "the little woman", as she sometimes refers to herself.

Now there has been another sewing delay that rivals the incident of the legendary pair of trousers that went in to be turned up. Two years later they emerged untouched and, miraculously, they fitted. With that protracted experience in mind, I decided to send another memo. Being a devout coward, I left this note out before departing hastily to work.

Memo to the little woman.
You will recall that I submitted my tracksuit bottoms to you for the elastic in the waist-band to be replaced. It ceased to do the job of holding the bottoms up during the warm-up session for a hockey match.

It is thanks only to the proportions of my stomach, a part of me which you continually criticise, that I was not embarrassed by the bottoms descending to ankle level.

It is fortunate that these past two months have been out of character as far as the weather is concerned. Had this not been the case, my lower torso would undoubtedly have been exposed on Saturday afternoons to the rigours of a British winter. I may well have fallen victim to a cold-related illness. I am sure that you would not want this as my input to the common good of Fortress H would be dramatically reduced.

I had been led to believe that things were progressing well. I was most impressed to find that within 24 hours of submitting the tracksuit for repairs, you had produced a new piece of elastic and removed the old. However, I am disappointed to note that there appears to have been no movement since.

The hockey season ends in April. May I respectfully ask if I will have the benefit of this garment before then? Indeed, would I be best advised to request a loan from the Fortress coffers and invest in a new one? At least I would then have a spare, should a further repair be necessary.

I will be quite happy to receive the repaired garment in lieu of a reply to this letter.

I remain your affectionate husband.

PS I understand the dry cleaners are of service of this nature.

I received a brief, scribbled reply contesting the length of the delay and insisting that I was never around when she wanted to measure me for the new bit of elastic. She replied to the PS, claiming that the dry cleaners are more expensive than she is. I thought about arguing with this. I reckon if we compare overheads there probably isn't much in it.

She finished her response with this: "Never have I been 'the little woman.' Petite, yes, but little woman, no." If it wasn't for the fact that my tracksuit is still awaiting repair, I would make mention of the jodhpur thighs.

Eastern Daily Press, Saturday, February 27, 1993

Hard to get a word in edgeways

Within just a few hours of the publication of last week's column, which told of the delay on renewing the elastic in my tracksuit bottoms, I spotted Mrs H heaving her sewing machine down the Fortress staircase. She lumbered it into the south wing and shut the door.

By the time I caught up with her, she appeared to be removing a film of dust from it. Seeing my stunned expression, she launched into a garbled explanation.

"I'm not having you turning up to hockey today and having a laugh at my expense because your tracksuit has not been mended," she said, with some feeling. I thought it would be better for me to turn up without it rather than have it seen that it took a newspaper exposé to galvanise her into action.

She measured me up and exacted some retribution for my revelations with one of her all too frequent digs at that part of me which had come to my rescue when the elastic expired.

"Gosh, we are going to need a lot of this elastic to go round your waist, aren't we?" Did I detect a note of heavy sarcasm in her voice?

At least, once she started sewing, there was an upside to all this. Such were the demands on her concentration that she became uncharacteristically quiet, and I and the Brats were left to drift rudderless for quite a while.

A silent Mrs H is indeed a rare experience. Oddly enough, I had received independent confirmation of this earlier that same day when I had visited the hairdresser who trims the locks of all the inmates. As the crimper snipped away, somehow we got on to the subject of shy people and how difficult it is to draw them out of their shells.

"It's difficult sometimes," she said. "I'll be doing someone's hair and they just don't say a word. Of course, I don't get that problem with Mrs H." Then she added hastily: "Mind you, I'd rather have it that way."

I was about to say that was all very well but she did not have to live with it, when I remembered that the scissors were flashing perilously close to my ears. Women do tend to gang up on us chaps sometimes, you know.

Indeed, Mrs H is never one to use two words where 15 will do. This greatly assists if she invokes the Fortress disciplinary procedure against me. I hate rows but as the verbiage is one way, all I have to do is listen. Unfortunately, this irks Mrs H and she demands a response. Otherwise, the matter would be closed as soon as she runs out of steam.

Brat Major also has an infuriating way of dealing with disciplinary situations. She employs this annoying tactic of bursting into tuneless song as she is being bawled out. If you do manage to make your point before she turns it into a musical her next trick is, the moment your voice dies away, to initiate a conversation with a third party in the room on a subject as far away from the bone of contention as possible.

She finds this most effective as Mrs H and I both rise to the bait. We soon end up eyeballing her with "Did you hear what I just said to you?"

"Yes - have you seen my ruler anywhere?" At this point she is dispatched to her room. No sooner has the door closed than the strains of Bobby Shafto drift down the stairs as she launches into a defiant recital on her recorder to let you know who is having the last word.

Mrs H and I almost had a row on Valentine's Day of all days. I offered to take her out for a meal. You'll never believe what the argument was about. I committed the unforgivable by asking her where she would like to go. Her view? It was up to me to make all the arrangements and simply take her out. The thing is, I know what she would have said if she hadn't approved of my choice.

Honestly, it's enough to make you reach for your recorder.

Loud and clear, the Brats are in action

I must start this week with an apology. Well, two actually, both relating to incidents in Norwich last Saturday. Firstly, if you were in the All Saints Green area around lunchtime, I am sorry if you were denied the conclusion of a rather loud pronouncement by Brat Major as her mother hastily cut short her comments in mid-sentence.

"If that lady's skirt was any shorter…" as she exclaimed her observation Mrs H grabbed her shoulder and neither the lady herself nor other passers-by knew what was in the young fashion expert's mind.

The second apology is offered to those enjoying a snack in the restaurant of a well-known department store. Fortunately, I was not there at this point but Mrs H has given me all the embarrassing details.

You will know which store I mean when I tell you it's the one where pigeons sit outside the windows. You will also recall the children when I tell you that one, the girl, was consuming a doughnut like it was her last meal and the boy was attempting to eat a cream cake, of which most of the cream was transferred from the cake to his left sleeve. Suddenly they espied two pigeons through the window.

"Mum, why has one pigeon got its beak inside the other's?"

Mrs H, intent on buttering a scone, suggested that one must be a young bird and was being fed. There was a short pause before those at surrounding tables had their attention drawn to renewed activity outside the window.

"Look what they're doing now! What are they doing, mum?" cried two excited voices in unison. Choking on her scone Mrs H hissed through her active teeth for them to keep their voices down.

"They're making love," she growled. The wiser Brat Major flushed slightly. Her brother, since the explanation had nothing to do with football, resumed his task of redistributing the cream from his cake to as much of his clothing as possible.

Perhaps it's the time of year that made these young pigeons' thoughts turn to billing and cooing. It certainly affects us. Spring heralds the arrival of the washing equinox at Fortress Haverson, and this alone caused last week's shopping trip to be delayed.

Throughout the winter, when the weather is damp, cold and horrible we need the heating on, the radiators are smothered with clothes that are either drying or airing. Mrs H also has a clothes horse which she stands in the bath. Not only do you have to heave it out when you want a bath but also stagger round with wet knickers slapping you in the face while you find somewhere to stand it.

Worse still is that, by spring, all the condensation caused by the damp breeds a healthy growth of mould. I have just harvested last year's crop when I decorated the bathroom.

Mrs H sets out to take full advantage of the "good dry" the milder windy conditions bring. This is fine except for one thing, which we experienced last Saturday before we embarked on our outing.

As usual, Mrs H was running late. Even the Brats were ready. Madame had finally agreed with her mother a mutually acceptable outfit. The young chancellor had counted his money several times and, whilst arriving at a different total on each occasion, had allocated himself sufficient funds to squander on some tape by an obscure pop group.

Both had even been persuaded to go to the toilet. Why do children fight against this so much before going out as if it is a matter of principle? The times we have got a few miles up the road and that pathetic little voice pipes up that they "just can't wait".

Anyway, there we were booted and spurred. The sound of Mrs H coming downstairs gave us hope of an imminent departure. Alas, when she hove in to view, it was not her handbag that she was carrying but a basket of washing and a bag of clothes pegs.

"Must just peg these out. There's a good dry today." Before we could protest, she pushed past with the comment: "Your jeans will only smell if I don't hang them out in the fresh air."

There are times when I would rather be a pigeon.

Sleepover? It's more like panic!

Mrs H has two speeds at which she operates around Fortress H. Overdrive and warp 9. If she ever exceeds warp 9 we know something is afoot. Last week I became aware that on occasions she was little more than a grey blur as she zoomed around the place at a speed approaching that of light.

Sure enough, she was limbering up for something. It was Brat Major's birthday. Thankfully, long gone are the days of the birthday party. Persuading them all to play The Farmer's in his Den and trying to stop the music at the right point in pass the parcel so the same person didn't get all the hidden chocolate.

And I remember vividly clearing up the aftermath. Collecting those disposable plates with gnawed sausage rolls and half eaten chunks of cake. Grinding crisps into the carpet with every step and stacking together the plastic cups, only to benefit from an unexpected shower of Coke thanks to one little angel who hadn't finished his drink.

We had the panic over the party bags, the bag of goodies which helps keep WH Smith in business, with all the pencils and rubbers they supply for such occasions. There were a few other bits and pieces included, usually edible. Mrs H always tried to add something a bit different.

For one of Brat Major's early parties she popped a couple of bath balls into each bag. These are the things you put in the bath while the water is running and they gradually dissolve into an oily fragrance.

"I wonder," I remarked casually as we bid the last guest farewell, "if any of the little dears will think those bath balls are sweets." Rarely have I seen Mrs H become absolutely motionless, then prove that she can accelerate from nought to warp 9 in a micro second.

She grabbed the phone and rang all the mothers and, with a voice bordering on hysteria, suggested that party bags should be searched and their owners frisked in order to establish that all bath balls could be accounted for.

We moved on to other treats such as ten pin bowling and this year, by way of celebration, the dear girl wanted the latest fad, a sleepover.

In case you haven't stumbled across this one, it means that friends come to stay the night and the rules are supposed to be relaxed. Curfew is extended and food, most of which is normally forbidden, can be consumed at odd hours without the risk of parental wrath.

Mrs H's increased activity was due to the impending day of the sleepover. The place had to be spick and span. This sort of thing always seems odd to me. Why go to all that trouble when three young ladies are going to undo all the good work? But I know better than to argue.

Mrs H wants everything just so. It's as if the guests are going to turn up with notebooks, survey the place and report back to their parents.

"The bedrooms were in an awful state. There were clothes everywhere and it didn't look as though she had dusted for a month. And I shouldn't think they possess a paintbrush judging by the décor."

As the day drew near, the atmosphere grew tense, and it wasn't just Mrs H. I strolled in one evening and burst into my rendition of Sailing, which I believe I perform far better than Rod Stewart. Brat Major responded as if someone had thrown a switch.

"Don't you dare do that when I have my sleepover," she exploded with more than a hint of panic in her voice. "It's so embarrassing."

The thought of being let down in front of her chums obviously worried her. On the eve of the sleepover a list of dos and don'ts appeared on the fridge door.

■ Don't sing at all anywhere in the house;
■ Don't call me any names;
■ Don't tell me off under any circumstances;
■ Don't tell my friends off or tell them what to do.
We must be allowed to:
■ Go to bed at midnight;
■ Have a midnight feast - not including Brat Minor;
■ Watch a video - without Brat Minor;
■ Have my music turned up as loud as I want.

Judging by the noise from the bedroom, the girls seemed to enjoy themselves. So much so that I thought there must be something in the sleepover idea. Choose your own food, do what you like. My birthday is not so very far away so I have informed Mrs H that, if she has no surprise plans for me to celebrate another passing year, I too will opt for a sleepover.

Dawn sparring at Fortress H

Each week Mrs H jumps in the car and embarks on a two-mile journey from Fortress Haverson to the supermarket. I can guarantee that not a trip goes by without her being the victim of "some idiot motorist". This stretch of road is peopled by a huge concentration of bad drivers, all of whom seem to have the avowed intent of disrupting Mrs H's journey.

"You should have seen the maniac in front of me coming back from shopping. Well, I don't know how I missed him. This van was turning left and some idiot in a silver car – don't know what make it is but it was like Cynthia's husband's mate's car. Anyway, he pulled out. . ."

It just amazes me how many traffic incidents Mrs H encounters. Now I do enjoy listening to Mrs H's motoring version of Jackanory. No, honestly I do, but I will admit there are times when I am busy but I try to show interest while continuing what I am doing. The trouble comes when I want to leave the room and she is still in full flow.

She trapped me in the hall the other day and the only way of escape was up the stairs. While she was holding forth, I began to move gradually up, step by step. I had actually made it to the seventh stair before she twigged and choked me off with: "You're not interested in this. Honestly, whenever I want to talk to you, you can't wait to get away."

But Mrs H is always one to turn a negative into a positive.

"If you're going upstairs, make sure they've put their school things out to wash, will you?"

To go and hassle the brats into putting out their dirty washing may sound an easy way out of listening to a Mrs H adventure, but it's not as easy as it sounds. Why do children have this block when it comes to getting their clothes washed? Their bits and pieces pile up in the bedroom but never make it to the laundry basket. They simply go to the drawer and put on something clean.

Well, that's not always true of Brat Minor. There have been occasions when a shirt has had to be put out of its misery by being ripped off his back before it begins to decompose.

And why do children have to do things in their best clothes? Brat Major was doing some cooking the other day. Mrs H gave her a good solid nagging over the fact that she was wearing her new sweatshirt.

"Don't worry, woman," said the teenage know-all. "I shan't mess it up."

Mrs H hates being called "woman", so when Brat Major's new sweatshirt subsequently turned up heavily stained, the ensuing eruption was like Mounts Vesuvius and Etna performing a double act.

I do put my things out to wash. My trouble is the way I do it. I am forever in trouble for leaving my shirtsleeves rolled up.

And then a couple of nights ago Mrs H let rip one of her truly handsome equine snorts as she was poised with the iron to press my pyjama jacket.

"Hurrummph! I do wish you'd undo the buttons," she complained. I protested that speed is of the essence in the morning and there really isn't time for such finesse.

Fortress Haverson is a place to avoid once the first alarm clock has sounded reveille.

I remember those times when we were tearing around the place because there were things the children couldn't do for themselves. Now they are more capable, I do believe it has got worse.

Brat Minor remains in his pit until the last possible moment. Even Mrs H who, if it was made an Olympic sport, could shout for Britain, cannot raise him with her penetrating bellows. It is necessary to physically eject him from his bed. Both offspring complain bitterly about the menu set before them for breakfast. It is not unusual for at least one of them to refuse food altogether. I wish they wouldn't, because we all get Mrs H's lecture on energy and raising the blood sugar level. At best, Brat Major may help make up the school lunchboxes but it depends on her mood. Brat Minor contributes nothing. It all becomes rather fraught, so I ask you – who has time to think about undoing pyjama jacket buttons?

The crunch comes when there is a cry from one or other bedroom: "I haven't got any clean school trousers." At this point Mrs H could not only shout for Britain but she could be a contender for the gold medal in freestyle daughter-strangling.

It's a good job Mrs H doesn't go to the supermarket straight after the dawn sparring at Fortress H. If ever she did, heaven help any of those motorists that get in her way.

Downtrodden husbands unite. . .

Throughout the years that I have been bemoaning my lot as a mere foot soldier at Fortress Haverson, there has been the occasional groundswell of support from those also serving a life sentence under the thumb. Back in 1991 I was made a member of the Society of Nagged Husbands. We didn't last long. Admittedly, there were only four members, but the odds against us were overwhelming.

Then there was Oppressed of Poringland. Do you remember him? He made contact by mailing plain brown envelopes to me containing tales of his struggle for survival and serving notice to younger hostages that things only get worse. Daughters, he warned, grow up and boss you about like their mothers do.

Oppressed told how he was allowed into the garden where he hid behind the compost container for a bit of peace and quiet. There were rumblings that we should all rendezvous there and compare notes. But resistance faded away.

Now another worm has started to turn. Frank Payne from Stalham has poked a tentative foot out of the closet. Frank is a printer and has produced some membership cards for what he calls the Fortress Haverson Club. The card proudly declares the club's purpose as being: "Especially for downtrodden husbands."

"These should be in the wallet of every thinking (or sinking) man in the area," says Frank.

Well, chaps, is this yet another cry for help? A plea from somebody who, like the rest of us, has somebody else pulling the strings? We need a voice. Perhaps the Fortress Haverson Club is the embryo of the revolution. If we are to have a club we must have a committee to run it. I am, therefore, inviting nominations for those willing to serve. Oops!

Sorry about the word serve. I didn't mean to make you twitch. I know the very expression creates stark images of the downtrodden lives we lead.

Let's start with chairman. This will be a very difficult job. Candidates will need the ability to control meetings and make decisions. Most of us are directed by others, and such skills have long since fallen dormant.

Of course, there will be a vice-chairman to step into the breach if the chairman is not allowed out. It should be quite easy to find someone for this post. After all, we are all used to doing somebody else's job.

"Get the door will you?" And "You answer the phone. If it's Celia, tell her I'll ring her back."

We shall need a secretary. This person will deal with our correspondence both by telephone and letter. Those with the right qualities will be easily recognisable. When their wife barks, "When you're in the city, just get me. . ." they will have paper and pen at the ready. They will be able to jot down a shopping list as it is rattled off and still be able to understand it when they get to the supermarket.

They will have the ability to think quickly. If they make a phone call to a club member and his wife answers, they will slip easily into double glazing speak. They will talk knowledgeably about barge boards until the phone is banged down.

Treasurer. Another important role. This has to go to a husband with a proven record of manipulating the housekeeping. Keep her in a manner to which she desperately wants to become accustomed, put food on the table and hang on to the price of the occasional pint.

He will have the difficult job of collecting members' subscriptions. He will need to be sensitive to those whose wallets are rifled regularly and need what little cash they can cling on to, to buy razor blades. As for the rest of the committee, well, there must be loads of us qualified for that. All we have to do is turn up and do as we're told.

Easy. We do it all the time.

We'll need a club motto. I suggest: "Who dares suffers." We will have a club tie embroidered with our emblem of crossed rolling pins. And we'll have guest speakers at our club nights covering specialist subjects such as: "Always have the right answer for your wife. Ten different ways to say 'Yes dear.'"

Ah, but where shall we meet? It must be somewhere that sounds convincing when we say we're going out. It'll have to be the office.

"Got to pop back into work for a couple of hours. Shouldn't be late." But don't forget to add: "Don't try and ring me. I'll be in a part of the building where we can't hear the phone."

I think we're almost there. Ink the roller of your printing press, Frank. We'll need loads of membership cards.

I wonder if he could make them with a magnetic strip. We could launch the Fortress Haverson Credit Card. Wouldn't it be great to have our very own flexible friend? Instead of just being one.

Had I known I'd have drawn up a prenup

I arrived home the other evening at the same time as Mrs H. We exchanged greetings, then walked silently down the path together. When we reached the back door, Mrs H wheeled round and fired with both barrels.

"Do you know, I was really put out today," she exploded. "When I came home at lunchtime they said on the radio that it would rain. Look at it now; it's been dry all afternoon." Then came the climax to this speech. "And I didn't put my washing out!"

Well, what could a chap say? I put on my best mortified look and made appropriate noises to convey my devastation at this cruel meteorological blow which fate had dealt Mrs H. Mentally I retraced my day but I could come up with nothing remotely catastrophic to compete with this.

I thought no more about this until a few days later when Mrs H was preparing the evening meal. I glanced at the clock and, to my astonishment, noted that we were still in the first half of the evening. All the signs were that my stomach could be in for a surprise with an early filling.

I spotted leeks and broccoli loitering on a chopping board, so I knew we were in for one of Mrs H's healthy dishes. The upside was that there was no sign of an aubergine.

I managed to escape from the kitchen without being pressed into service. From a safe distance I listened to the sounds of chopping, sizzling and stirring. I was summoned occasionally to do the odd bit of washing up but generally I got off lightly.

Finally Mrs H announced that the meal was but a few minutes from being served. I was getting out the eating irons when a giggling Mrs H suddenly appeared.

"Guess what?" she chuckled. "I've forgotten to do the potatoes!" Driven by an empty stomach my answer was immediate.

"I'll go without," I insisted. "I am not waiting while you do potatoes. Gimme bread, gimme anything instead but I want my food!"

Gosh, I'm so assertive when I'm hungry.

"Do you know, that's the first time I've ever done that," mused Mrs H.

Either, for once, I got my own way or Mrs H was hungry too for we ate a potatoless dinner.

Later that night I was reading the newspaper. Now, if it hadn't been for those two incidents, I probably wouldn't have paid as much attention as I did to the article on prenuptial agreements. Of course, this buzz phrase wasn't in existence when Mrs H trapped me. We put our names to the traditional agreement; for richer for poorer, in sickness and in health and all that.

But had I known what I know now, prior to the attachment of the ball and chain I may well have drawn up a document, detailing a few safeguards. Here are a few sample clauses:

■ Either party may conclude a conversation if they find it irrelevant and of no interest. For example, detailed descriptions of the trip round the supermarket giving up to date prices ("you should have seen how sprouts have shot up since last week") may be terminated with, "I'm going to clean the car".

■ As the car is driven by both parties, it is perfectly acceptable for either to insert petrol, oil and water. Cleaning of said car should be done as soon as it is dirty not left to see who cracks first.

■ It should not be assumed that just one of the parties will be responsible for the washing up. It is not obligatory to make phone calls immediately after meals, you know.

■ Either party may do the garden. Access to the shed is unlimited and there is no restriction on who may operate the lawnmower or perform the ancient skills of digging and weeding.

■ There is nothing to say that the party who chooses the paint for the walls shall play no part in applying it.

■ Responses to such questions as "What do you think of my new skirt" shall be taken at face value and not assumed to have a hidden meaning like, "you're just saying that to shut me up".

■ Failure to return from the pub at the declared time is not sufficient grounds for the party left at home ironing to refuse to communicate in anything other than Neanderthal grunts.

Unfortunately I am closing the stable door when the horse has long since bolted. I learnt very early on in our married life that Mrs H had already drawn up her own prenuptial agreement.

Mind you, it's not the actual agreement I have trouble with; it's all the penalty clauses.

Perhaps we're not such bad parents after all

In the eyes of her children, Mrs H swings between being a "control freak" and a "health freak". They claim that if she is not forcing them to eat a diet loaded with salad, wholemeal bread and fruit, she is subjecting them to a lifestyle riddled with restrictions.

Brat Minor became quite militant, refusing to eat his packed lunch, his defence being that he is not allowed anything he likes in his sandwiches. We asked him if his mates ate their sandwiches. And of course they do.

"They're all allowed jam."

We had all this at the Middle School. Mrs H used to send both the younger inmates to school with a packed lunch which included a bit of salad, usually a well-scrubbed carrot. This attracted a variety of rabbit jokes, so Mrs H eventually relented and the carrot was saved for them to consume at home.

Now we're going through it all again at the High School. To compromise, Mrs H has made another major concession; she has allowed white bread in the house. But still Brat Minor would return home with his food untouched. We thought we were making progress when, occasionally, the lunchbox was handed in empty. But his downfall came when he lost something, and I was invited into his squat to help him look for it.

There are not the words in the English language to describe the advanced state of decomposition of the banana I liberated from his desk. Fortunately, the ham roll was mummified in cling film so, unlike the banana, surgery was not involved in removing it from its hiding place.

Brat Minor was given Mrs H's lecture in maintaining blood sugar levels and how food would give him energy. "No wonder you flop out in front of the television when you come home. You've got nothing inside you to keep you going."

Mrs H imposed a fine on her son, making a small deduction from his pocket money.

"I'm not wasting money on good food. Perhaps if you have to pay for it you'll eat it!"

Currently a fragile treaty is just holding, with Brat Minor agreeing to eat his rolls providing he is allowed to drench the filling with pickle. By placing all these outrageous restrictions on our children, Mrs H and I believed we were unique as parents.

But then we received a tremendous boost. It came from Brat Major in a brief appraisal of our current performance as parents. Her pronouncement means we may have been knocked off our perch as the parents from hell. For the truculent teenager to concede such a point is indeed a high accolade.

It started a few months back when she began going to teenage discos. For her, it was a bit like being let out on parole but with the added obstacle that she had Mrs H for a parole officer. These sorties into the big wide world involved the truculent disco dancer being subjected to intense questioning from her mother before a pass was granted.

"Right, I want to know who is going with you. What time does it start and what time does it finish? Your father is taking you, who is picking you up? What are you wearing? Not those new trousers I hope. You can see your knickers through them! And do not leave the hall – I don't care if the others nip out for a burger, you stay put!"

If she were to be believed, on the evening of the disco, every teenager will desert the village. All of them will be allowed to stay out as late as they like, and they will go flush with huge sums of money with the girls wearing the skimpiest of outfits.

The journey there is quite revealing. Usually, there are three if not four of them in the car. The radio is tuned into a chassis-rattling station, but I can still pick up the odd snippet of conversation.

I've learned that so and so is grounded and someone else isn't allowed to stay out that late. Yet another one has to stay in because relatives are coming. I stored this up until the next time Brat Major accused us of draconian parenting.

"Hang on," I said. "What about these others that aren't allowed to do the things that we let you do?"

Then she said it. "Well, you haven't been quite so bad lately."

It was like winning an Oscar. Boosted by this, we felt confident enough to approach our daughter when we spotted her in the city shopping with friends. We were greeted with a square-jawed bout of truculence.

Mind you, as we pointed out to her later, while she was busy scowling her mates chatted happily to us.

But this, she explained, was fuelled by nothing other than them thanking their lucky stars. "You see, it's because you're not their parents."

Silence is golden – unlike Brat Major's pizza

It always seems to happen when I make a cup of coffee at work. I settle down at my desk, have a quick slurp, bury my teeth into a ham roll – and the phone rings. One day last week, I was ravenous. I took a huge bite out of my roll and, sure enough, the wretched instrument warbled. Like a true professional I swallowed my half-chewed food – together with my annoyance – and, trying not to choke, answered in my best customer-friendly manner. I was greeted by a rather impatient voice.

"What time will you be home tonight?"

"About 6 o'clock." I replied.

"Do you want a cooked meal?"

"Oh yes please," I said gratefully.

"I'll do toad-in-the-hole. See you later, Bye."

I know what you're thinking. Mrs H has finally come to her senses. She's going to be more considerate to the poor old chap; have his grub ready when he gets home. Well, it's a nice thought; but I'm afraid you're way off beam. The call was from Brat Major. Her brother was having an operation on his foot. Mrs H was at the hospital with him, so the Truculent Teenager was in charge of catering and clearly taking her job seriously.

The first meal she had served was a bit of disaster. The dear girl had taken the easy route and got a pizza out of the freezer. She put it in the oven for the stated time and gave me strict instructions to be available in 27 minutes.

I heard the timer go and headed eagerly for the kitchen. This was a treat, I was going to have tea at teatime.

Brat Major extracted the pizza from the oven and, drawing on all her culinary training, she performed the crucial test to see if it was done. She stuck her finger in the middle of it.

It was cold. We checked the instructions, but she'd done everything by the book. It had to go in for a bit longer. It failed the finger test for the second time, so she subjected it to yet another bout in the oven. But it showed little response to further treatment so she subjected it to a quick blast in the microwave.

Eventually it succumbed. Well, the middle was perfect – but we did have to battle bravely with the outside, which was erring a trifle towards the crisp.

As Brat Minor was a bit groggy, Mrs H decided to stay the night at the hospital so I found myself plunged into a rare freedom warp; one of those brief spells where Fortress H becomes rudderless and I can come and go as I please. I crawled into bed that night and settled down – in absolute silence. Oh how I missed hearing the day's closing headlines. There was nobody to ask me what the weather forecast was for the following day, and then curse because she had nothing appropriate to wear.

And goodness knows how I got to sleep without the sporadic background sounds of cotton wool being extracted from the packet, the tops of preservatives coming off and being dropped on the dressing table while a good squirt of the contents was squeezed out and slapped on.

The following evening I arrived home, eager for my toad-in-the-hole. Guess what; more shades of Mrs H. It wasn't ready. I managed to raise the cook from her lethargy, and she prepared the meal before disappearing to continue doing what bored teenagers do.

I was left to do the potatoes and veg. I ended up bolting my meal before changing and rushing to the hospital. As I was about to leave, Brat Major demonstrated yet more frightening traits of her mother.

"And what time will you be home?" she demanded.

I answered – just as I would if Mrs H had asked me – in a way that was less a statement, more a seeking of permission.

"About nine?" I said tentatively.

I arrived on the ward and plonked myself in a chair. Mrs H greeted me in a way only she could.

"Humph! Those socks are the wrong colour to wear with those jeans."

I tried to point out that it hardly seemed worth changing socks for a couple of hours, but Mrs H pointed out that it was decisions such as this which were standing in the way of me becoming a fashion icon.

Meanwhile Brat Minor was looking exceedingly seedy. He and anaesthetics do not get on. In fact, his face matched the plaster on his leg. It seems that no longer does it come in white only, there is a choice of colours and he had selected a fluorescent green. It looked as though he had been exposed to nuclear waste. He's at home now, with his leg up on the settee. He is lying around watching television and doing very little while we wait on him.

Nothing new there, then.

Ink in My Blood

I could table a written question

I walked up to Mrs H the other day, bent forward and laid my head on her shoulder. "What's all that about?" she demanded. "Just a spontaneous gesture of affection," I replied.

"Humph," she scoffed. "That's what the cat does."

"Yeah," I responded animatedly. "And look what you say to him. 'Hello my treasure' and then he gets fussed."

"Yes, well he's a cat, you're not."

Sometimes I think Mrs H is just so busy that she doesn't have time for me. Why the Mog doesn't fall into this category I am at a loss to explain. I don't dig up the carpet, I don't turn my nose up at the food she serves me and I have never plucked her best top with an extended claw. But when did you hear Mrs H at the back door calling plaintively: "Neil, Neil. Where are you my treasure?" Then bang a can of beer with a mug to entice me in.

There are those occasions when I am bursting to tell Mrs H some news but something has popped into her mind and it has to be said. She presses some form of over-ride button and, even if I am in the middle of a sentence, her thoughts take priority. It's like the announcer's voice when it cuts into a television programme.

"We interrupt this programme to go over to the newsroom for a newsflash."

I was babbling excitedly the other day about how hard I worked in the garden. This triggered something in Mrs H's mind which took precedence.

"I've dug all the front borders and …"

"Did you clear the leaves out of the drain?"

I decided to plough on regardless.

"And I've done some of the back …"

"Did you clear the leaves out of the drain?"

"Next I must kill all that moss in the …"

"Yes, but did you clear the drain? I have to say these things while I think of them."

I confirmed I had cleaned the wretched drain and was about to carry on a rundown on my gardening achievements so I could bask in the inevitable praise, but Mrs H simply picked up a pen and began writing something on one of her endless lists. I gave up, but seeing her scribbling away did prompt an idea. What about communicating like they do in Parliament sometimes?

You know, when there isn't time to raise something during a sitting, they table a written question. I could leave a note out at breakfast time and there would be an answer in the evening. I may even get a verbal reply as part of the early evening headlines.

"The Right Honourable Member for Lower Fortress asks if there will be any possibility that he could skive off to the pub this evening. I must advise him that contrary to there being any thought of recreational activities there remains the outstanding job of putting two pictures up in the bedroom. May I remind the Right Honourable Gentleman that these were taken down around two years ago and I have been campaigning for the restoration of hanging ever since."

But I have my uses, as I proved last Saturday. I entered the bedroom to find Mrs H looking out of the window at Brat Minor and a brace of Interlopers. I had retrieved the garden furniture from winter storage. As soon as Brat Minor and his mates spotted the table and chairs on the lawn they adjourned to the nearest supermarket where they purchased a small barbecue and enough food to feed the five thousand.

After a certain amount of angst they succeeded in assembling the barbecue and set about cooking their food. Fortunately, by the time they reached this stage we had gone out. I have no doubt that, had Mrs H witnessed their attention to hygiene and their less than rigorous checks to establish that the burgers were thoroughly cooked she would have reacted like Gordon Ramsay on a bad day. But the point is, having eaten and washed it all down with lager, they became bored. The barbecue was still smouldering so they thought it would be a spiffing good wheeze to chuck on the odd twig that was lying around, a legacy of one of my savage bouts of pruning.

Mrs H observed the flames from the window and ordered me to the garden to tell them to put out the fire. Obediently I presented myself before three whooping youths and advised them that Mrs H required them to extinguish their furnace.

To my amazement they agreed, but when I got back in the house Mrs H greeted me with: "Well, did you tell them? It's still burning."

I insisted I had and, fortunately, the fire was soon put out. Had it not been, I had a mind to resort to Plan B and invite the Right Honourable Lady, the Member for Upper Fortress, to do it herself.

A bargain that came in handy

T he babbling brook gushes busily over millions of rocks. Eventually it will wear them smooth. Likewise, I think any remaining resistance I may have had to Fortress rules and regulation over the years has been gradually eroded. Mrs H has been doing the babbling and, maybe once, I was a chunky rock; but now there are signs that I have been smoothed into shape.

The realisation came when I was sent on an emergency shopping trip. You can imagine the desperation; we were out of kitchen towels! A list was thrust in my hand with: "Perhaps you could just get these few things, but we really are desperate for kitchen towels."

I know that we don't have patterned kitchen roll. I do agree with this. I can't see the point in spending more on something with daisies on when all we're going to do is grab a sheet to mop up spilt coffee. But suddenly, I found myself examining the labels, calculating the number of sheets per roll in relation to the price.

Having, in the past, spent what seemed like hours, leaning on the trolley while Mrs H does this, on solo runs I usually exercise the policy of get in, grab and get out.

When I got home, I bore them into the kitchen as if I had shot them in the bush and was going to mount them on the wall in the north wing. Unfortunately, Mrs H wasn't there to share in my triumph so I stashed them in the cupboard under the stairs.

I forgot about them until later that evening when Mrs H emerged from the cupboard with the giant pack of paper towels slung over her shoulder as if she was delivering coal.

"Suppose these were cheap, were they?" she growled. "Can't store them under the stairs, it's not hygienic."

And I thought I'd get brownie points for the savings. They are now sitting upstairs in the spare room like an artefact on display. Maybe Mrs H is creating a museum of Haverson howlers.

But I must stiffen my resolve and make sure I don't cave in to all of Mrs H's regulations. Worryingly, there are signs I am being beaten into submission over the Mog. Some years ago, I declared that, if a cat was to be taken on the

Fortress payroll, I would have nothing to do with its maintenance. Well, there are even chinks in my armour here.

I complained when his food was upgraded from tinned to sachet. Well, to my horror, I find I am now feeding him regularly. Brat Minor used to make sure the Mog had breakfast but, now he has left, somehow the job seems to fall to me. I'm even obeying Mrs H's edict to "wash his bowl".

This is tedious first thing in the morning – and is enough to put me off my muesli. Brat Minor would heap fresh food on top of the remnants of the previous meal. Mrs H does get worked up over this.

"How would you like to eat your tea off a dirty plate?" she used to challenge Brat Minor.

"Wunt care," he would reply. And he probably wouldn't. In fact, now he is in his own gaff, I would say the probability of him eating off used crockery occasionally is quite high.

But I have to say that this has caused my relationship with the Mog to mellow ever so slightly. I am afforded a rub of his head on the ankle while I dispense his food. But that is as far as it goes, and I stick to my view that, as far as I can see, he serves no useful purpose.

Last week, Mrs H sent me out to remove a dead bird that we can only assume the Mog had caught. I complained but Mrs H sprung to his defence.

"You can't blame him, poor little chap is only following his instincts. Mind you, I have been worried he might have worms, but he didn't eat any of it."

It was then that I spotted something at the bottom of the stairs. Realising what it was I opened my mouth to speak, but Mrs H was in full flow.

"Anyway, I've told you he's good for my blood pressure." And then she saw it too. "Oh no! He's been sick."

"Yep," I cackled. "Not such a 'little treasure' now is he? He gobbled down his food, marched into the hall, threw it up then headed for the armchair where he is now asleep as if nothing had happened. He's your cat; I'm not clearing it up."

We still have the Fortress sick kit. This was introduced when we had a cat that would vomit at will. In a bucket is a plastic bag containing an old spatula, a pair of rubber gloves, a sponge and a cloth.

With an expression on her face as if she had just eaten something nasty Mrs H set about the task of clearing it up.

I was cock-a-hoop.

"Need any paper towel?" I chortled. "We've got plenty."

Flushed with embarrassment

I had one of those moments the other day when I was confronted with a situation for which the brain simply can't come up with a solution. A feeling of mild panic wells up in the pit of the stomach and the mind crunches options like someone playing a fruit machine in search of that elusive jackpot.

My desperate situation occurred in the new Norwich Chapelfield development last week. The whole issue of this new shopping centre is bad news for any husband. There are now so many shops in Norwich that, what for me is a fractious marital trawl, could be something that travel agents offer as a short break.

Mrs H decided that we would carry out a reconnaissance of the potential credit card swiping that was available in the new centre. It was to be a swift tour on the understanding that she would blitz the place at a later date with her goss 'n' shop mate while I remained within the confines of Fortress H doing chaps things like painting skirting boards.

Our journey of discovery started out well as we joined masses of people purposefully marching towards what appeared to be nowhere. As is the case with Mrs H and me, the smell of freshly-brewed coffee lassoed us and we were soon taking caffeine on board to sustain us through the rest of Mrs H's reconnoitre.

Inevitably, after a large coffee, the loo was the next thing on the agenda. There are strict rules here. We can't both go at once. One of us has to play minder to the carrier bags while the other seeks relief. Mrs H went first. When she emerged, she informed me that, if I went in a cubicle, the locks were stiff with newness.

"I nearly panicked!" she said. "If a girl in there hadn't warned me I'd have been really worried."

I breezed into the loo. There were two cubicles, one engaged. I dived, so to speak, into the other. I was just about press the flush when something made me freeze. I could hear the sound of voices; female voices.

It took just a nano second to register. So that's why there were no urinals. I was in the ladies.

At this point the brain reclassified the situation from routine to utter terror. I bought a bit of time by delaying pressing the flush.

In what seemed like hours but was probably only 15 seconds, I wracked my confused brain for a solution. Nothing rational came to me.

Perhaps they'd just go away. Unlikely. Perhaps whoever was in the other cubicle would come out and the rest would go en masse into it and I could slip away.

Should I use my mobile to contact Mrs H and summon her to my rescue? But what would she say? "Excuse me, my husband's in there. Do you mind if he comes out?" Besides, there was no signal.

The female chatter continued. I knew there was nothing for it; I had to face it out. I flushed the loo, took a deep breath and burst out of the door. I was greeted by two ladies who, I have to say, looked decidedly unfazed to see a male erupt from their loos.

"Ha ha! I'm in the wrong loo!" I practically shrieked with hysteria. Then I thought, if in doubt, blame Mrs H. "I'm awfully sorry, my wife said go in and turn left. I did and here I am," I continued in a voice a good octave above the norm.

Fortunately, they just giggled. And I didn't give them time to reply as I crashed Tom and Jerry-style through the door. I sought sanctuary in the proper gents where I swiftly washed my hands.

I zoomed back to Mrs H.

"Grab the bags quick!" I hissed. "Let's get out of here before those ladies come out of the loo."

High on adrenalin, I led a bewildered Mrs H into the crowds. She must have wondered what on earth I had done.

When I thought it was safe, I stopped and related my experience to her. She did, of course, think it a great hoot but reversed my falling stress levels by speculating what might have happened if the ladies had not seen the funny side.

At that point my mobile rang. What! Had they tracked me down?

But it was Brat Major, as ever wondering if we were anywhere near a shop and if so could we just get…

I was still not fully in control and before I knew it I had blurted out the story to her. I realised that was a mistake as knowledge of my plight was no longer contained and, no doubt, in the retelling, the story would receive some embellishment.

Ink in My Blood

I was more or less calm by the time we arrived home. Brat Major was just leaving Fortress H.

"So the toilets in Chapelfield are a bit dodgy," she mused.

Hmm, nothing wrong with the toilets; just those who use them.

Mind you, perhaps they could make those little pictures on the doors a bit bigger.

Eastern Daily Press, Saturday, February 25, 2006

An alarmingly personal question

I've had what you might call a challenging weekend with Mrs H. Oddly enough, I didn't do anything wrong. In fact, things got off to a reasonably good start.

Mrs H was getting ready to go out, I was pacing the corridors showing the usual dogged patience when I strayed into the bedroom. Instead of the usual: "If you leave me alone I'll be ready much quicker," it was the equally frightening: "Well, what do you think of this?"

I was momentarily puzzled, as she was wearing a top that I had seen many times before – but auto-pilot kicked in.

"Yes, that looks absolutely fine."

"Hmm, I thought so," she said before adding, "I don't often wear this necklace."

Necklace? Not the top then. Good old auto-pilot came to my rescue again.

"It'll make a change then," I said brightly.

Phew! That was close. But I got away with it and, just before we left, I did even better.

Mrs H fixed me with her defiant look and said: "I haven't used the straighteners on my hair. I think it looks all right as it is. What do you think?"

"It looks lovely," I said enthusiastically.

Okay, that was a bit over the top.

"Phworr!" scoffed Mrs H. "You've never said that before."

"Right then, we'd better get going," I babbled in a bid to change the subject.

I thought I may have scored some brownie points but, as we made our way around the city, an even greater test presented itself.

If you were in All Saints Green on Saturday afternoon, you may have spotted a woman break into a run until she was a few yards ahead of her partner, then look challengingly over her shoulder. This was Mrs H and me.

We were following another couple when Mrs H grabbed my arm and said: "There, look at her. Is my bum as wide as that at the top of my legs?"

Just what do you say? I chose my words very carefully.

"Er dunno," I whimpered. Come on autopilot; where are you?

"How am I supposed to tell?" I said at last. Phew, another close one!

"I'll get ahead so you can compare," said Mrs H breaking into a gallop and speeding up behind the other woman.

I was confronted by two posteriors. The owner of one was looking at me over her shoulder with a steely stare. The owner of the other, thankfully, was blissfully unaware that she was the subject of scrutiny.

And remember that what the casual observer would see was a solitary male walking behind two women staring fixedly at their posteriors. Almost grounds for an ASBO.

But what on earth was I going to say? Rather than shout an opinion to Mrs H I decided to wait until I caught up with her. This gave me thinking time.

"I would say," I began measuredly, "that you are both about the same – and neither of you are big," I added hastily.

Silently, we followed the other couple into a store with both Mrs H and I having eyes fixed on the woman in front. I felt obliged to say something.

"You know you're not that big there," I protested. "You haven't got the jodhpur thighs anymore."

This brought the second big "Phworr!" of the day.

"Had them since I was born!" she snorted.

The subject was dropped. We had gone to buy a travel alarm clock and arrived at the counter. This simple transaction paved the way for Mrs H to get her own back for any errors of judgment I had made that day.

Mrs H is not at her best first thing so, when she gets up, conditions have to be just right. This includes an alarm that does not cause her to levitate to the ceiling. It was, therefore, a prerequisite of our purchase that Mrs H listened to the bleep of the alarm before she parted with any money.

We chose two clocks and asked an assistant if we could set the alarms off. The combined brain power of the three of us failed to get either clock to work. Two more sales assistants were summoned, and between the five of us we managed to get an assortment of bleeps echoing round the store. Mrs H was impressed with a quiet start that built up to a crescendo if the drowsy owner does not hit the snooze button. It took a good 15 minutes before Mrs H made up her mind.

When we got home, I set the time on the clock and gave the alarm a quick burst.

"I thought it started quietly and got louder," said Mrs H.

"That was the other one," I replied.

"Oh no!" wailed Mrs H, "I don't want that one."

On Sunday morning, I headed dutifully back to the city to exchange the clock. I got home with the replacement and gave Mrs H a burst of its alarm. She let out a horrified gasp.

"Oh no! It didn't sound as loud as that in the store."

Arrrgghh!

If she'd asked me then how big her bum is…

Eastern Daily Press, Saturday, July 14, 2007

When Mrs H bit her tongue 'hilence his halmost holden'. . .

Now, don't snigger at what I am about to tell you. It's not funny. Although I have to say, when Mrs H told her shopping mate about it, she did rather chuckle.

Okay, take a deep breath and grab something solid. Last week, Mrs H bit her tongue so badly she was unable to talk.

Oh now come on, I said it wasn't funny. I mean, poor old thing was in agony. I found her in the bathroom twisting her head this way and that as she tried to inspect the damage in a hand mirror. When she saw me she opened her mouth as wide as she could, pulled back her lips, thrust out her tongue and invited me to have a look at the injury.

I must say, it was not a pretty sight and I'm not surprised she was in pain. You don't realise just how lethal teeth can be until you do something like that. But there was an upside, for me though. I was able to get away with murder.

She did try to maintain smooth running at Fortress H but I couldn't understand much of what she said. And, no, I wasn't being obtuse. I didn't deliberately misunderstand her.

As if.

Telephone calls to Fortress H were probably the shortest since records began. Either Mrs H was unable to take them, so callers were treated to a brief chat with me, or they listened to Mrs H snorting down the line at them and quickly gave it up as a bad job.

After a day or two, I did become quite expert in translating her Neanderthal grunts. To avoid jaw movement, which obviously hurt, these were delivered via the nose, with most words prefixed with an 'h'.

"Hust he if huh hat his hare," translates as "Just see if the cat is there."

"Huh hoodness hake! Ow hany himes have hi hold ew hot hugh oh outhide hin hoar hippers?" was Mrs H speak for: "For goodness sake! How many times have I told you not to go outside in your slippers?"

When she bit into her tongue she was eating; something that became almost impossible from that moment on. To maintain nourishment, the Fortress menu had dishes on it that required little or no chewing and would find their own way down the throat with the minimum of swallowing.

Mrs H likes her food, and I knew she was pretty bad when she cancelled a meal at her favourite Italian restaurant with her shopping buddy.

I was dispatched to the chemist to find something to dull the pain.

It was with some difficulty I looked the pharmacist in the eye and said: "My wife has bitten her tongue and can't speak. Can you recommend anything?"

There must have been a hundred and one answers to this question but, after the faintest twitch of the lips, she became serious and produced some gel that contains anaesthetic which would numb the area temporarily.

I hastened back to Mrs H who was going about her duties with a set expression on her face. She had fixed her jaw in a position which caused the least grief. Until, that is, she applied the gel. Then she had a look on her face as if she had just eaten an Aubergine Bake with the aubergine long past its bake-by date.

"Ass hohhible!" she announced through her nose. "Hi hink hi'll high hargling wiv halt hater."

(Translated, that was: "That's horrible. I think I'll try gargling with salt water.")

Over the next day or two her tongue began to heal. She was able to get words out but ended each sentence with a howl of pain.

"I need the potatoes peeled now!

Aarrrrghhh!"

It took several days for the healing process to allow Mrs H to return to normal. And then she made up for lost time. There was so much to be said, so much had been bottled up for days. On one occasion we were watching a film on DVD. Out came those famous words.

"Just pause it. I want to get my slippers. Oh by the way…"

It was almost three-quarters of an hour before we got back to the film by which time I had lost track of what was going on.

Mrs H still has the odd wince. You know how it is; once you do something like that, you are forever catching it, usually when you least expect it.

As I write, Mrs H is preparing a fulsome meal. After days of soups and soft fruit it is a relief to be back on solids. And I'm sleeping better. I'm not being woken in the early hours by a strangulated yelp as Mrs H turns over and swallows in her sleep.

It's good to have Mrs H back in full voice. Life at Fortress H was quite strange while she was tongue-tied. It was most uncomfortable; a bit like Stockholm syndrome where the victim shows loyalty to the hostage-taker.

Eastern Daily Press, Saturday, April 26, 2008

Wedded bliss is tested while decorating the kitchen

Yet another milestone has passed since the formal attachment of the ball and chain. The years have absolutely flown by. I know I was single once. I've seen pictures.

To mark the occasion I did the rounds of the shops to find a card appropriate for Mrs H. Most of them contained words like: "With you I have found somebody I want to spend the rest of my life with."

Words like "stable doors" and "horses bolting" came to mind. Since I've already spent more than half my life with her it seemed a bit late for that.

Perhaps I should have made up my own words.

"We've been together all these years
But my love it isn't flinchin'
Mind you we almost came to blows
Over that flaming kitchen"

As it happened, our wedding anniversary coincided with the finishing touches being applied to the kitchen. The workmen have gone and there are only a couple of outstanding jobs to be done and we're there.

Apart from the decorating.

Oh no, here we go again; another round of colour matching and a multitude of test pots. At least I have done the ceiling, that was no contest when it came to colour – and you can imagine our paranoia at the danger of getting emulsion on the new units. Before I was allowed to take the lid off the paint Mrs H began covering everything in sight. She used plastic dust sheets, taping them to the top of the units and draping them to the floor. By the time she had finished, the room was totally enclosed in plastic.

I switched on the radio, poured out the paint and wriggled into the plastic cave. Mrs H vanished on some other mission and I settled into that semi-comatose state that overcomes you with the rhythmic rumble of the paint roller.

Suddenly my reverie was shattered. The Fortress kitchen leads into a small dining area; this also has to be decorated. There is some preparation work to do here and Mrs H was going to get on with this. I don't think I'd noticed before - I certainly should have done after all these years - but Mrs H talks non-stop while she works. I listened from within my plastic cocoon. The radio took second place.

Her first job was to fill a crack in the ceiling.

"Does this filler need stirring?"

"Yes, use the spatula."

"What spatula."

"The one on the window sill," I said directing her to the plastic filler knife I had got out specially.

"That's not what I call a spatula. I think of a spatula as something I cook with."

And then the commentary started.

"This filler's not sticking very well in this hole. It's too gloopy; I can't stipple it like the rest of the ceiling. Reckon we'll have to paint it and see what it looks like. I may have to go over it again. I don't know what to do for tea tonight. We can't use the kitchen. By the way, did I tell you…are you listening to me?"

"Sorry dear, just doing a difficult edge."

The next move is to get the kitchen fully functional, but all those things we hadn't thought about are rearing their heads. Mrs H has spent hours staring at empty cupboards wondering what to put where. I keep out of the way, but if I forget myself and happen to wander in I am expected to contribute.

"I don't know whether to put the spices on this shelf or that one. And if I have the cutlery in that draw, where do we keep the things like spare tea towels? What do you think?"

Quick; think on feet.

"Well…why don't you put the spices up there?"

"That's ridiculous! I use the spices a lot. And I can't reach that shelf without a stool."

"Er…okay. I'll just go and clean the paintbrushes."

Part of the trouble is my old maxim of familiarity breeds acceptance applies. Things that weren't satisfactory in the old kitchen we got used to and they became the norm. With the new one it's different. These gremlins have been ironed out but new ones have taken their place because we're not used to them – if you see what I mean.

For example; the aroma of a stir-fry hangs around the house for 24 hours. Now we have an extractor over the cooker.

"I don't like this!" exclaimed the cook. "I'm going to bang my head on it when I lean over the stove."

My thoughts go back to Christmas when we were stuck in a massive queue at the supermarket. We found ourselves passing the time with the chap behind us. The subject of kitchens came up.

"If I had to choose one appliance to keep in my kitchen," he said, "it would be the dishwasher. I can manage without the rest."

For the first time we have a dishwasher. But because we have never had one there seems no urgency to work out how to use it. There it stands, pristine, waiting to release me from the Marigolds. I can't wait.

Already I'm looking at it and saying: "With you I have found somebody I want to spend the rest of my life with."

I haven't forgotten my food – yet

Recently I revealed that the Fortress Mog had reached his 13th birthday and that he is not quite as supple as he was. He rallies when marauding mogs invade his territory but, generally, he moves at rather a sedate pace.

But it's with his food we have noticed that maybe it's not only his joints that are getting creaky; we think his mind is going as well.

One morning last week I put some food in his bowl. When I arrived home he was pacing around the house wailing despairingly as if he had not been fed for weeks.

I tend to ignore him when he does this, but his mistress is more sympathetic.

"For goodness sake stop wailing. I'll feed you in a minute. NEYULL! Can you feed him please?"

On this occasion Mrs H did respond to his lobbying. She had been shopping and was putting the cat food away. Hearing the sound of the cupboard door the Mog took his wailing to new heights and shuffled up to see if the familiar sound meant food was in the offing.

Now, this shows how sad thing are; Mrs H showed him two boxes of food – and began to discuss the contents with him.

"Look there's rabbit and duck – and you like the fish in the jelly, don't you?"

She extracted a packet and he milled arthritically around her feet as she headed for his bowl. And here's the rub. When she got there, she discovered there was still half a bowlful left from the morning.

"Look!" she exclaimed. "Did you forget this was here?"

Clearly this had slipped his mind. He sidled up and began happily eating. Once he'd had his fill he sauntered off, heaved himself on to the sofa and slept for the next five hours.

Unfortunately, I am not in a position to comment on displaying the signs of ageing – neither for that matter is Mrs H.

On a week's break in Derbyshire we reflected on our holidays when we had Brats M and M in tow. How we spent the days begging, pleading and cajoling them into walking up hills and around stately homes. In return they were allowed to feast on things that were banned from the Fortress larder.

We steeled ourselves to join them in canoes, on bikes and white-knuckle theme rides. Mrs H was constantly on red alert.

"Sit still! You'll have us all in the water."

Oh, what we would have given to escape to the pub in the evening to unwind. But with two slumbering youngsters to babysit, we just watched telly, read and did the crossword before psyching ourselves up for another round of stress the following day.

But here we were with no ties and a county bulging with pubs offering untested ales for me to sample.

But we'd been out all day and were staying in the middle of nowhere, and simply couldn't be bothered.

One day we decided on a restaurant for an evening meal. We headed back to our cottage to change. I was first to articulate our thoughts.

"I don't really feel like going out," I said tentatively.

"Neither do I!" Mrs H exclaimed – with a hint of relief in her voice. She added: "You know what? We're getting old."

How sad is that? All those years of having to take holidays in the peak period; cafés, car parks and pubs were heaving, parents shouting at truculent children and children whinging at "controlling" parents. And there we were… watching telly, reading and doing the crossword.

And, like the Mog, I must confess the joints aren't as well-oiled as they once were.

But I have yet to forget I haven't finished a meal.

Mind you, I might use that trick next time an Aubergine Bake pops up again on the Fortress menu.

Eastern Daily Press, Saturday, July 11, 2011

Such a proud day for the father of the bride

I checked my watch; time to make a move. I was under orders to be at her room at a quarter to two. It was time to do my duty. Mrs H issued her final instructions to me. "Tell her to look up, smile and walk slowly."

With a perfunctory "Yes dear" I set off to collect the bride.

I tapped on the door and pushed it slowly open. There were the three bridesmaids; they looked fantastic in their sumptuous purple dresses.

And there she was; my daughter, in her ivory wedding dress. She looked absolutely amazing. And around her neck she wore her Grandma's pearl necklace.

Something old.

This was the girl I'd scooped up when she was small. We'd built snowmen, played in the sandpit, splashed in the paddling pool and dug the garden together. I'd read a library full of books to her. I'd driven her to sleepovers, dance classes and, more latterly, nightclubs. Mrs H and I have shared in her successes, comforted her when the going got tough and nursed her when she was ill.

I hugged her.

"Air kisses only – you'll mess up my make-up."

It was almost two o'clock, time to go. We made our way nervously to the ceremony. Through the door I could see friends and relations standing in eager anticipation; and that was when it really hit me. I was about to give my little girl away.

"Look up, smile and walk slowly," I hissed.

"Okay," she whispered back. She hasn't always taken my advice so readily. We made our measured way to her waiting fiancé. She did look up, she did smile – and I only had to check the speed of our progress once.

I delivered her successfully to her future husband. Someone we know will look after her and treasure her as we have.

"Who gives this woman?"

"I do."

I took my seat. In a flash she was married and we were facing the camera for the photographs.

And then there was my speech. Fathers of the bride trawl through their daughters' lives telling selected anecdotes. What could I say? Most of Brat Major's exploits have been published in this newspaper.

I did take the opportunity to warn the groom of a couple of points; if he hadn't come across them already. I suggested he would be well advised to do what he was told when he was told.

When she was about four, we were packed to go on holiday when we heard a bloodcurdling scream from Brat Minor. His sister had slammed his fingers in the door. We asked her why she had done it when she could see his hand was in the way. She said simply:

"I asked him to move it – and he didn't."

Toasts were drunk. In his speech the best man touched on some of the groom's finer moments. The whole day went like clockwork, a tribute to Brat Major's careful planning.

And what about Mrs H? After that traumatic search, she did find an outfit that was in every way mother of the bride. And she looked stunning!

But there was an eleventh hour panic. The evening before the wedding I found her with the bed covered in pairs of tights. There must have been seven pairs.

"I can't wear any of these," she wailed. "These ones are too orangey, these ones are too shiny – and these are so tight round my waist they hurt!"

Thank heavens for late-night shopping. Within minutes we were in the car and heading for the shops to purchase more pairs of tights.

Okay, I know I'm not the first father to give his daughter away but I just wasn't prepared for such an emotional experience. I defy any bride's father not to admit to a lump in the throat; to a moistening of the eyes . . . and, most of all, a feeling of unbridled pride.

Eastern Daily Press, Saturday, January 12, 2013

Going back to my teenage years

Apparently my life is in the process of going full circle. Mrs H has informed me that she is rather concerned that I am demonstrating all the traits of turning the clock back to my teenage years.

"Honestly!" she exploded. "Every time I try to talk to you, you've got your head buried in your mobile. What are you doing, for goodness sake?"

But that's not all. She is compiling an ever-lengthening list of things I do that are typically teenager.

"You walk out of the room and leave the telly on, there's music blaring out all over the house but you're in the garden. Think what you used to say to the children when they did that!"

I'm sure this is the natural cycle of life. From the innocence of birth you develop over the years to maturity. Then you peak and plunge into the downward spiral.

By the time that great fortress in the sky beckons, you need all the care you had when you were a baby.

If that's the case, I might as well enjoy it while I can.

If I'm starting to behave like a teenager, why not go all the way? We've always resisted having a TV in the bedroom.

That will have to change. As I adopt my reclusive lifestyle, it will be essential.

I have no doubt I will be dispatched to the spare room.

We will need to invest in additional crockery to ensure a continuous supply for my constant eating. Plates coated with a variety of food that has set like concrete will be strategically placed around the bedroom, with old crisp packets stuffed under the bed. No need to put dirty washing in the laundry basket; just leave it strewn around the bedroom.

And, of course, I won't have to communicate with Mrs H – other than in monosyllables and the odd rant.

"Tea's ready. Have you washed your hands?"

"Uh. Whuh is it?"

"It's aubergine bake.

"Phww! Want pizza."

I shall be staying out late, staggering in noisily around 3am. I shall not emerge from my pit until the early afternoon, at which point I will occupy the shower for some considerable time, using the entire tank of hot water.

No longer will I have to ask Mrs H anything. I will know it all.

Money will be no object, and if I want to go out, there'll be Mrs H's taxi service.

Suddenly I have a new respect for my children. They were right all along. Why did I get so worked up when they were sullen and uncommunicative? Why did I resist their demands for money?

And why did I force them to go on holidays that didn't cost them a penny.

Watch out Mrs H, hermit Haverson is in the building.

The boot's on the other foot as the children pay a visit

Last week we had a visit from our children. Firstly, Brat Major came to dinner one evening after work. Admittedly she was using Fortress H as a motorway service station, but it had benefits for me. She was meeting a friend at 7pm.

Mrs H groaned: "I suppose I'll have to have tea ready when she gets here."

I arrived home from work to a rare scene. I was greeted by the smell of cooking. Mrs H was flying around the kitchen. Somehow, without the help of her faithful kitchen labourer, the evening meal was almost ready.

By 6.30 we were seated at the table eating. Brat Major glanced across the table at me and said wryly: "You don't normally get your tea this early."

After she'd gone, the evening stretched out ahead. What should we do with all that time? Mrs H filled it without trouble and we didn't sit down until our usual time.

"See," she said triumphantly. "All I've done is do everything I normally do before tea, afterwards."

Last Saturday Brat Minor came for the day. He was on a callout to sort our electronic problems, so we thought we'd take him out for lunch.

He joined me in the hall for the pacing ritual while we waited for Mrs H to get ready. We were summoned to offer an opinion on her new top.

"Both of you come and look," she instructed.

"Looks good," I said and headed for the door.

"WAIT!" she bawled. "I want a young and an old opinion."

Both of us made appropriate positive comments.

"Are you sure?" she asked. "You're not just saying that because you want to get away for lunch?"

With that she turned to the side and bowled us a real googly.

"How does that look? Is it too short so it emphasises my saggy bum?"

Well, I ask you, what do you say to that – and stay friends over lunch?

"Nooo, not at all," we answered in one voice.

But there was more. Mrs H was wearing different boots on either foot.

"Well?" she demanded, proffering alternate feet.

Brat minor was quicker off the mark than me – and braver.

"If I were you, I'd wear the same boot on both feet," he said with that endearing hint of sarcasm of his. "And don't wear the shiny ones, they look like something out of Saturday Night Fever."

Mrs H snorted but seemed satisfied. At last we could get off to lunch – well almost.

"Hang on! If I'm going to wear this new top I need to cut the label out."

That is the final confirmation it has gained approval and will become a permanent item in Mrs H's wardrobe.

But I know what will happen. At some stage in the future she'll get it out to wear and curl her upper lip.

"You know, I never was happy with this top. I think it makes my bum look saggy."

Eastern Daily Press, Saturday, March 22, 2014

She's showering me with advice while I just dry up

We were in WH Smith looking for a greetings card. Suddenly Mrs H turned to me and unceremoniously pulled down my zip. Hang on, not that one. The one in my jacket. She thought I should have a more casual look. I didn't argue. Currently, Mrs H is riding high in battles of a marital nature at Fortress H.

It's not that surprising, she's nearly always right, and when she's not, she isn't usually wrong. She scored a major victory over me in the incident of the shower.

There are a number of things in the home I could live without if I had to, but the shower is something I really savour. I think this dates back to my sporting years. Coming off the hockey field on a freezing January day and wallowing in a hot shower was sheer bliss.

We didn't have one at home in the early days, so when finally we had one installed, I'd use every excuse to hop in. A spot of gardening or a clammy summer's day was all it took.

So, imagine my horror when I spotted paint bubbling on a wall that backed onto the shower. There was a leak somewhere in the pipe work. Immediately Mrs H put the shower out of bounds until it was repaired.

To me this was the equivalent of giving away my last Rolo. I put forward an argument to keep the water flowing.

"But it will only leak when we have it on," I protested. "When it's turned off, the water will just sit there. If we're careful we could still shower occasionally until it is fixed."

Mrs H was not convinced. She insisted it was the other way round. Turn it on and the additional pressure would increase the leak.

We had a protracted and tense discussion about it.

"I don't understand what you're saying," Mrs H insisted.

I said the same thing again – and again.

"But I don't understand your explanation," she insisted.

"Well," I huffed. "I can't explain it any other way."

The plumber arrived, found the leak and announced it was terminal. We needed a new shower.

"I'll turn the water off," he said. "If it's left on it'll keep on leaking."

Mrs H punched the air in triumph.

"YES! I told 'im it would," she exclaimed, jabbing a finger in my direction. "He wouldn't have it."

"Well," I babbled desperately. "I just thought if the water had somewhere to flow it wouldn't leak."

But I was defeated. I took it like a man – until a couple of days later when Mrs H, buoyed by her triumph, returned to the subject and lectured me on making myself understood.

"If you have a point of view, explain it, don't just clam up!"

Now our roof has sprung a leak. I've been in the loft, but I can't find where the water is coming in.

And I am not offering an opinion.

From the mouths of babes – and stroppy teenagers

When Brat Major first started school, the head teacher made a deal. At the introductory evening she said: "I'll only believe half of what your child tells me about you if you'll only believe half of what they tell you about us."

I recalled this when we decided to do some de-cluttering and began sorting through Brats M and M's school work. We're halfway through Brat Major's. It's just wonderful. So far we've read almost every word she wrote and there are some gems.

We asked them if they wanted their school work, but both were utterly dismissive of it. We'll keep some of it. I'm sure when they get older they'll enjoy reading their take on their childhood.

At the First School, on a number of occasions, Brat Major wrote in her school diary: "I went shopping with mummy. We bought apples, oranges and bananas."

In accordance with the deal, hopefully the teachers didn't think we lived on a diet solely consisting of fruit. Although there is an entire entry devoted to her hatred of sprouts.

When she was a bit older she wrote movingly of a field trip: "I missed mummy and daddy." But then added: "And maybe my brother."

On a visit to Sherwood Forest, we made the mistake of buying Brat Minor a bow and some arrows. In her diary, his sister documented his attempts at archery.

"He practises with his bow and arrow but keeps missing the board and hitting me."

I have no doubt this was due to his erroneous aim and was in no way deliberate.

Reviewing their growing years gave us both a warm glow. Inevitably we fast-forwarded to the teenage years. Looking back, we laughed at some of the memories, but boy, at the time, they really wound us up.

We remembered their infuriating rejoinders. One of the most irritating was the combining of two letters to produce a word that caused my blood pressure to soar.

"You still haven't done your homework."

"So?"

This later expanded into a sullen: "And your point is?"

But one of the memories I treasure most is Mrs H's reaction to the incident of the tomato soup. Brat Major was around 15 at the time. She marched into the kitchen sporting a surly teenager scowl.

"Woss for tea?" she demanded.

"Home-made tomato soup," Mrs H replied, clearly pleased that she was giving her children home-cooked, wholesome food.

"Leave me out," said the snotty teenager, as if she'd been offered a meal of raw sprouts.

With that, she went to the cupboard and extracted a tin – of tomato soup.

With what appeared no physical effort, Mrs H levitated from her seat and all but adhered herself to the ceiling.

We have since talked of these occasions with Brat Major, reminding her of what she was like as a teenager.

"Well," she sniffed. "Turned out all right in the end, didn't it?"

There was only one reply. "And your point is?"

Eastern Daily Press, Saturday, September 12, 2015

Like father like son, well maybe

Last month Brat Minor and Catherine did the family rounds before moving to Derbyshire. I thought the lengths to which Mrs H went to prepare Fortress H and feed them before they moved north could not be surpassed.

I was wrong.

Last weekend they came to Norfolk for a wedding and stayed a couple of nights with us. I was mobilised like never before. I had the week off prior to their visit. Mrs H drew up a schedule detailing what would be done on which day. Shopping, rooms to clean, beds made up, towels washed and aired; you name it, everything was allocated a slot.

By Thursday evening I'd had enough.

"That's it. Tomorrow I am not picking up a duster or firing up the vacuum cleaner."

Surprisingly, Mrs H agreed. In fact, I think she mentioned the word "chill".

Then Friday morning just before they were due Mrs H said: "Could you just run through with the vacuum?"

"No!" I replied defiantly. "I said I was not doing any housework today."

Mrs H's sympathy from the night before had evaporated.

"You've done one bit of intense housework!" she exploded. "I've been doing it for years. Now you know how I feel. You do a piece of your work and it's there forever, housework has to keep being done."

Suitably chastised I heaved out the vacuum cleaner. By the time Brat Minor and Catherine arrived the place was immaculate.

On Saturday morning Catherine picked up the EDP and read about Fortress H. She fixed Brat Minor with a steely eye.

"That's where you get it from," she said. "Your sarcastic comments when I ask you what you think of my hair or what I'm wearing.'"

I'm not sure which of us was most put out, me or my son. The time for them to depart for the wedding drew ever closer and there was no sign of Catherine. Brat Minor was getting agitated.

"I've lived with this for years," I said. "It'll only get worse." Apparently, they just beat the bride to the church.

The subject came up again the following day. Honestly, it could have been Mrs H and me.

Catherine confided in me: "He's just like his mother. He's never ready when we are going out." Brat Minor appeared, having overheard. He came out fighting. "It's not me, it's you," he protested.

"Just as we're ready to go, you decide to go to the toilet," Catherine responded.

"I've already been once. But I've been waiting for you for so long I have to go again."

The argument began to heat up.

"All right," Catherine asserted. "I'll go out with no make-up. I won't do my hair; it can mat into one long dreadlock."

Maybe it's a sign of the foundation for a lasting relationship. I should warn my son that eventually he'll be beaten into submission. No, perhaps I'll let him find out for himself.

I had to.

Weighing up the chance to get one over on Mrs H

I don't weigh myself often enough. Maybe I don't want to step on the scales and see a reading that proves everything Mrs H says about my eating habits is right.

Last week I had a good excuse not to weigh myself. Mrs H announced that the digital display in the bathroom scales went blank. She had put some new batteries in but nothing happened. She thought the batteries might be in the wrong way so she turned them over. Still nothing.

"We'll have to get some new scales," she announced.

Amazingly, the scales came with a 15-year guarantee – and we'd only had them a couple of years. But among all the terms and conditions it said that in returning them, we had to pay for postage and packing both ways. They weren't that expensive, so it wasn't worth it.

Mrs H went on one of her procurement exercises, checking websites, reading reviews; we even visited a few shops to see what was on offer.

Finally she made a decision on which scales she wanted and where to get them from.

I was surprised that the scales had packed up. Out of sight of Mrs H I slipped in the new batteries and, hey presto, they sprung into life.

To get one over on Mrs H is rare. These victories are all the sweeter when she has tried to do something and failed, then I step up and it works.

I slipped it nonchalantly into conversation.

"Oh by the way, the scales are working okay."

"What! But you watched me put new batteries in."

"Yeah, but I wasn't looking closely."

Mrs H accepted defeat graciously – but she wasn't on the back foot for long. An opportunity for her to strike back soon presented itself. She had inspected the corner of Fortress H where I retire for some solace.

"You room is disgusting!" she said with real feeling. "Come with me," she added in a voice that had me following her obediently.

"Look at this, and this," she said running her finger into remote corners of bookshelves where dusters aren't designed to penetrate.

"I did clean in here," I protested weakly.

"Phworr! You wouldn't know it. Did you use the yellow thing?"

There are at least three different "yellow things" in the cupboard. There are yellow dusters, something that looks like a truncated version of Ken Dodd's tickling stick and a long flat sword-like weapon for hoiking out dust from under such things as washing machines.

"Yes," I replied with an obvious lack of interest. I didn't want to get into a debate about yellow things.

Not satisfied, Mrs H gave me a quick tutorial on removing dust from and around books. Armed with this new knowledge the problem should be solved. And things have just got even better.

As I was writing this column Mrs H's head appeared round the door with some life-enhancing news.

"By the way," she announced proudly. "There's a new yellow thing in the cupboard."

Eastern Daily Press, Saturday, December 12, 2015

A book before bedtime? No, we play the maracas!

While we've been decorating Brat Major's old room, Mrs H's closing headlines have featured paint, duvet covers, curtains and carpets. The closing headlines, you will recall, are a review of the day's goings-on at Fortress H which Mrs H delivers as I am drifting off to sleep. I hang in there as best I can, but she gets a bit shirty if she slips in a question in the middle of the bulletin and all she gets for an answer is a distant grunt.

Sometimes it is difficult to drop off. Before she assumes the position at her dressing table to slap on the preservatives there is an awful lot she has to do. I can identify some of what she's doing from the racket. She sorts clothes that she's just ironed. This involves opening and closing drawers and the rattling of coat hangers. It's a bit like having someone in the room playing the maracas.

The hooks of hangers cross each other on the rail, so when she pulls one out half a dozen escape at the same time.

"That's right, all fall out why don't you?" Mrs H explodes.

Here I heave a huge sigh.

"It's all right for you. You can just get into bed and go to sleep. I've got masses to do."

Occasionally, the closing headlines are interrupted with breaking news.

"Oh no! I'm almost out of cotton wool. Remind me to put it on the shopping list. Did that compute?"

One evening this week, Mrs H excelled herself with a real nugget. I was almost asleep when she came out with her "And finally…"

"You don't get carrier bags when you buy clothes any more so I've got a John Lewis top that I've got to take back and it's in a Marks & Spencer's bag."

Even Mrs H recognised the banality of this gem.

"That's hardly riveting is it?" she added.

The overwhelming need for sarcasm snapped me out of my reverie.

"Gosh that's pretty serious. I do hope you get the right shop?"

Mrs H responded with a dismissive snort and switched the light out. This signals the end of the news and that she is off to pad around the house until well after midnight.

When she finally comes to bed, the window may have to be opened or closed down a bit more, depending on the weather, and there is a final application of some cream or other. Occasionally, she drops the top of the pot with a resounding clatter.

Within minutes of getting into bed Mrs H is out cold. I am now wide awake. Immediately I think: do I want to go to the loo? That's fatal.

The thought is in my mind and, regardless of whether I want to go or not, I have to haul myself out of bed.

But maybe here's a chance to get my own back as I lumber in the dark. But Mrs H doesn't stir.

Perhaps I should get some maracas.

Eastern Daily Press, Saturday, February 26, 2016

Want to stay fit and attractive? Just follow Mrs H. . .

I read in the paper the other day what yet another celebrity does to keep fit, slim and attractive. Don't they realise that – as I've been telling you all for weeks – the real way to a healthy life is to follow Mrs H's tips? Okay, she's not a national celebrity though I consider her slim and attractive.

There, that should keep the Aubergine Bake at bay for a week or two.

I am delighted to report that she has added another exercise to the ones I've already shared with you. Let's quickly recap.

There's standing on one foot while you clean your teeth. This helps with balance. In fact, Mrs H does this at random. She will jump up in the middle of a TV programme and stare at the screen while standing like a bewildered stork.

This takes care also of the issue that Mrs H has read about that every hour you sit watching television knocks 20 minutes off your life.

And we mustn't forget singing 'Happy Birthday' twice while you wash your hands.

Last week Mrs H was again banging the drum about the lack of exercise we do.

"We must make a point of going for some long walks," she declared, before adding: "I'll tell you what else we'll do. Come to the table and sit down."

We were in the kitchen. Fortunately, it is at the back of Fortress H so no one passing could see what happened next.

"Right, stand up and sit down 20 times – and don't use your hands to help yourself up."

So there we were, two mature adults facing each other across the table, springing up and down like jack in the boxes.

Mrs H is the one who's good at maths but I thought I could at least count. I finished what I thought were my 20 while she bounced up and down another four or five times.

"That's more than 20," I complained, joining in again.

My knees were protesting but Mrs H seemed to be rising from the chair with ease.

Part of this exercise has been enshrined in daily Fortress life. I am supposed to rise from the armchair without using my arms to propel myself.

Apparently knees, hips and stomach muscles all benefit from this. Just think, you could make a circuit out of that lot. Every hour, make 20 no-hand attempts to get off the sofa, sprint to the bathroom, stand on one leg and wash your hands while singing Happy Birthday.

Mrs H does have another exercise. She hasn't inflicted it on me yet. If she pops say, some milk in the microwave for a couple of minutes, she will pound up and down stairs while it's heating. I have tried it; it's a killer. It's really painful above the knees and leaves me gasping for breath.

Now, if you're planning to get fit, you'll need a personal trainer.

I know just the person.

Let's Talk
magazine
2002-

We all have views on life. On some issues we feel strongly about, with others we go with the flow. For over 15 years I have been in the privileged position of having a page in Let's Talk to put forward my own point of view. Here is a selection which were published under the title of The Last Word. But that often went to the readers who I am relieved to say, more often than not, agree with some of my politically incorrect thoughts.

The good old days: were they that good after all?

You know, I vowed I'd never say to my children some of the annoying things my parents said to me, but I do. I can't help myself. "We never had that when I was young," I say heavily. "Here we go again; the good old days," comes the sneering reply.

When I lapse into cliché mode it always brings to mind that classic '70s hit from Gladys Knight and the Pips, The Way We Were. Remember it? The lyrics sum it all up so well.

Gladys sings that the good old days were a time: "When life was slow and oh so mellow. Winters were warmer, the grass was greener."

Well, was it really? Were things better than they are now? Or has everything gone into soft focus and we only remember the good bits?

Here's another snippet of Gladys' wisdom: "Bad as we think they are, these will become the good old days of our children."

So, where we talk of having no fears in leaving the back door unlocked and ruminate over getting a joint of beef for two and sixpence, what will our children see through their rose-tinted spectacles? Will they go dewy-eyed over these days of street muggings and getting a rather different joint for the price of a hot mobile phone?

Maybe the pace was slower and the streets were safer years ago, but I'm not convinced I would like to hop in a time machine and live through, say the late Fifties or early Sixties, again.

Take creature comforts; these days most of us have central heating and double-glazing, we can move around the house on a winter's evening without noticing a change in temperature. Well, what about those days of a coal fire in one room? If you went to the bedroom you had to put your overcoat on.

My mother used to make draught excluders out of old stockings stuffed with material. These were laid in front of the doors and along the windowsills to stop the warm air escaping through ill-fitting sash windows.

Now here's a topic to stimulate conversation in the pub: is central heating responsible for the demise of the vest? I wasn't allowed to go to school without one. I wouldn't be seen dead in one now.

And I shudder at the thought of the food we ate at my grandparents — particularly in summer. No fridges; meat, butter and milk were kept in the pantry in a 'safe', a small wooden structure with a vented door. All right, the flies were kept at bay but I do wonder sometimes how long things had been in there and at what temperature.

There were no 'Best Before' dates to give a clue — and certainly the food wasn't riddled with preservatives.

Mind you, I don't remember any of us keeling over clutching our stomachs having feasted on grandmother's Sunday roast.

I wonder what Gladys Knight makes of it all these days. She's still singing, but I believe she's minus a Pip or two now. As she concludes in that song of hers: "If we had the chance to do it all again, tell me, would we? Could we?"

Well, would you?

Five bad things about the "Good old days"

1. No VCR. So I couldn't record Z Cars, Quatermass or The Army Game.
2. No screen washers on cars. A friend carried a Squeezy bottle and leaned out of the window to squirt the windscreen.
3. Twin tub washing machines. Remember heaving soaking wet garments from the washing part into the spin dryer with huge wooden tongs?
4. Shorter pub hours. Some hostelries didn't open until 7 pm — and they closed at half past 10!
5. Gritting the roads. The council scattered sand on the packed snow, they didn't use salt. Rear-wheeled drive cars skidded all over the place.

Five good things about the "Good old days"

1. Steward & Patteson's bitter — I remember it at around 1/11d a pint.
2. No mobile phones — and you could put four pence in the box, press Button A and talk for as long as you liked. It was always worth pressing Button B when you did hang up; sometimes you got your money back.
3. Spangles! Tasty and easy to slip into the mouth during a maths lesson. I was forever fishing the stripy wrappers out of my school blazer pockets.
4. The train. Before Dr Beeching wielded his axe, you could travel by rail to most towns in Norfolk without having to drive — and it was affordable.
5. If you did drive, parking was easy — and cheap.

Let's Talk magazine, December, 2002

'Watney' ever happened to our traditional drinking houses?

// What?" exclaimed my father. I could almost hear the cogs of his brain turning. "That's ... that's three pints!" I'd just returned from the annual general meeting of Swaffham Cricket Club which had taken place in the Elizabethan Room above the King's Arms. I was aged 16 and had my first brush with beer.

Something in my manner had clearly alerted my father to the fact that I had been drinking and he was interrogating me to find out to what extent. With the disarming honesty that alcohol induces, particularly in a novice, I confessed to having "Siz bols Wonney brown".

With great mental dexterity my father divided six by two and came up with the three pints.

I didn't stay on Watney Brown for long. I graduated to Steward & Patteson (S&P) bitter; some used to say there was more P than S in it. It conditioned my palate for life. I blame the cricket club. As I got older and became a regular member of the team, not only did I settle into my game but also I adopted the ritual of a visit to the pub.

Once the clearing up had been done and the pavilion locked it was "see you up the K.A." We always drank in the bar. In fact, in all my years frequenting this alehouse I can only remember setting foot in the lounge once. It was somewhere we just didn't go.

But a gradual change began to take place in our pubs. First it was the beer; hand pumps disappeared, Watney swallowed up the local breweries and made a full assault on our beer drinking - who remembers the slogan "Bitter's on the move to Starlight"? This was Watney's clumsy ploy to wean us off real ale on to fizzy keg beer.

My drinking habits changed too; a woman entered my life. I found myself in lounge bars. Instead of leaning on the bar I learnt to sit at a table and sip a pint instead of quaffing it. Suddenly I was ordering strange drinks like Martini and lemonade - and if she wanted a short, well, my wallet flinched; it was twice the cost of a pint!

Mind you, that's all changed now, there's not much difference in price these days.

Not satisfied with attacking our beer Watney gutted some of our finest hostelries, knocking bars and lounges into one room. They had a plastic feel and an overbearing red hue.

Having left Swaffham, I often wondered what happened to the K.A. I made a sentimental return recently, and it was with some trepidation that I entered the door, wondering what fate had befallen my inaugural watering hole.

The door to the bar was there, but it took me into one large bar. Maybe it was my mind, but the old character I had known engulfed me. The ghosts were coming out of the woodwork.

Landlady Julie Parker and husband Nick listened patiently while I rambled on at some length about how it looked in those days when a pint of S&P was 1/11d. There's a carpet on the floor now and a full menu is available. That's a million miles from my time when salted peanuts were added to ready-salted crisps (thus doubling the range of food on offer).

There was the alcove where the dartboard used to be: "We've only just taken it out," said Julie. And the Elizabethan Room where I broke my drinking duck? Yes, that's still there too.

I sighed as I left, wallowing in the memories of days when the worst crime most 16-year-olds committed was a few Watney Browns.

Let's Talk magazine, August, 2004

That's it – no more whinging

Right, let's be positive this month. All I seem to have done in the past few columns is whinge. Well, this month I'm coming from the perspective that the glass is half full, not half empty. Instead of knocking life today and banging on about how good things were years ago, I'm going to restore your faith in the 21st century.

Now, I've had plenty to say about the quality of service we get these days, so let's start with a shopping experience. I went to the chemist to pick up a prescription. The girl foraged on a shelf and produced a paper bag containing a bottle of some evil mixture intended to prompt a certain part of the digestive system into action – not mine I hasten to add. Sorry if that's too much information, but there's my first positive. In grandma's day you'd probably have had to rely on a few helpings of prunes to start the cycle.

No. I'm not going to say the problem wouldn't have occurred in the first place because, back then, everybody ate more fresh vegetables. After all, that would be a whinge. Anyway, as I stretched out a hand to take the package, the girl whipped it from my grasp and thrust it under the counter. She disappeared, returning seconds later with the same prescription minus its paper bag.

"There you are," she said. "It's cheaper to buy it over the counter." My mouth went into goldfish mode as I grappled to find the words to express my spluttered thanks. All right, it didn't save me mega bucks but, as a well-known supermarket proclaims, every little helps.

Ah yes, supermarkets. They've been a target of my vitriol in the past. Well, while the person for whom the bowel-loosening brew was purchased was unable to do the weekly shop, yours truly stepped into the breach. Armed with a list, I blitzed the aisles as if I was competing in that Robot Wars on TV.

I zoomed to the checkout with a trolley spilling over with items, about three quarters of which were actually on the list. I loaded up the conveyor belt and stood eagerly with my first carrier bag poised to pack.

"Do you want any help with packing?" asked the girl on the till.

"Nah, thanks," said macho man with more confidence than he felt.

Things started hurtling towards me. I stuffed them furiously into carrier bags. I was falling behind the flow – and I have to admit I wasn't exactly applying much science to my task. Eggs were wedged under cartons of fruit juice and a large container of disinfectant. And there was a distinct possibility that the bread might have a taste with more than a hint of non-biological washing powder. I will admit that some of the delay may have been caused by the care I took in placing four bottles of much cherished beer in the trolley.

Suddenly, I became aware that the goods were arriving ready loaded in carrier bags. As she bleeped them through the till the dear girl was packing them – sensibly. There was a hint of a smile on her lips which said: "Men! Why are they so useless?"

She pressed the button to print out the receipt. This seemingly endless piece of paper sprouted from her till. It would have challenged the hardiest of Andrex puppies.

"Thank you for your help," I said, pathetically, as I signed the credit card chit.

"You're very welcome," she said, in a tone that suggested she had stopped short of patting me gently on the head.

It was a humble Haverson that piloted the bulging trolley to the car park. I wrestled everything into the car boot and vowed that in future I would be more generous to my fellow humans. I wasn't going to be labelled "a grumpy old man".

On the journey home, I gave way gladly to other motorists. The next day I stood very patiently in the Post Office queue as the dear lady in front fumbled in her cavernous bag for an elusive tax form. I even managed a smile when the lawnmower wouldn't start. Mind you, I never had that problem with my old push mower. And I didn't have to dash to the garage to buy a gallon of petrol when I was half way through mowing.

Ooops, there's a hint of a whinge there. Oh, what the heck, I'm sure I'll feel better if I get all the grouses off my chest. And I bet I won't have to visit the chemist to err...get things moving.

Let's Talk magazine, September, 2004

What will future generations make of 'political correctness'?

Do you have to pinch yourself sometimes to persuade your brain that what's going on around you is actually happening? Some things seem so bizarre they defy belief – but we jog on through life as if it's all par for the course.

Take some of the things that have become banned for fear of litigation. Children can no longer play many of the playground games that we grew up with, in case they get injured and the school is sued. And did you read about that nurse who got thousands in compensation because she was allergic to latex? In my book that's tough. She's just not suitable for the job. But the courts found the health authority had a "duty of care" and she has all that money – and she can go to work somewhere else and earn more.

We have a quick whinge about it all, but generally we take things in our stride and move on to the next barmy outpouring.

Now, you may find this incredibly sad, and be moved to suggest I get a life, but I often fast forward 400 years and try to imagine what those inhabiting our overcrowded planet in, say, 2404 will think of loopy life in the 21st century.

Flip that on its head and look back 400 years, and see what you think of what the establishment was inflicting on our ancestors. We would now be eight years into paying the Window Tax. I mean, what was all that about? If you had more than six to nine windows you had to cough up a couple of bob to help pay off the debts caused by raging inflation. Imagine that being introduced now. Instead of your tea being interrupted by calls from double glazing companies touting to fit new windows, you'd be canvassed by brickies offering to fill them up!

But don't laugh just yet. Did you know that the Window Tax replaced the Hearth Tax? Seriously. It was becoming fashionable to have fireplaces in the mid-17th century and the government had to find a way of paying the million pounds plus they had allocated to the King, so they whacked a two shilling levy on every hearth in the house. It could cost quite a bit to provide a warm spot for granny to sit and crochet.

But back to 2404 and there you are zooming along an aerial M6 in your Skoda SupaShuttle tuned into Radio 4 – yes, nothing will change the BBC – listening to a history programme on 2004.

What's that they tell you? A prisoner got his foot caught in a shower drain hole and was awarded almost half a million pounds. Gosh, what wacky times they must have been. Didn't they have any common sense? Oh of course not, someone called Lord Falconer* banned the use of the phrase by the judiciary. Apparently, so he reckoned, it meant different things to different people. Bet he was the life and soul of the party.

And there was the man who chased the car thieves and apprehended them. They got a suspended sentence and he got convicted of GBH. Hmm, maybe the worthy Lord was right. There is no such thing as common sense.

I must admit there are certain phrases I would be happy never to hear again. "Breach of human rights" is one that has me gagging with angst. Throw in an "emotional trauma", add a touch of "post-traumatic stress syndrome" and I could cheerfully kick the cat. I wouldn't of course. Might offend those nice people from the Animal Liberation Front.

Some day soon, we may see the back of that dreaded phrase that has me reaching for the TV remote quicker than when Big Brother comes on: "Weapons of mass destruction". It's even been afforded its own abbreviation,

WMDs.

I guess one of the most frustrating things is that I am forever reading comments from people saying: "This is political correctness gone mad." But nothing seems to change. In fact, if anything, it seems to be getting worse.

I wonder if it will be any better in 2404. I suspect not, just different. There will be a tax on the number of computers in your house, fast food will be a small tablet containing all the ingredients of a Big Mac and they'll still be arguing over the Euro.

Now, if you've taken offence over anything I've written this month, don't you dare sue. After all, that would be a breach of my human rights.

Arrggghh, I said it!

*Lord Falconer was Secretary of State for Justice from 2003-2007.

Let's Talk magazine, December, 2006

Out to lunch, at the double

Working a stone's throw from the shops leaves me exposed to being sent on regular buying missions during my lunch hour. Actually, I don't mind that much; I treat it as a constitutional and I try to walk briskly rather than slouch along.

But sometimes an hour is barely long enough and at times I end up at the gallop. I rushed out of a shop the other lunchtime, furiously juggling with a loaded carrier bag and a handful of change. Despite my best efforts three pound coins plunged to the ground and made good their escape in different directions. I bent to pick them up. Now, I've reached that age where bending down is invariably accompanied by an involuntary grunt. I know this; I accept this - although I do put it down partly to being a bit overweight as well as the result of advancing years. But what happened next did make me feel old.

I had retrieved two of the miscreant coins and, as I grovelled in pursuit of the third, I psyched myself up for the rise to the perpendicular. Before I could get to the coin a slender hand snaked in front of me and scooped it up. I looked up to be met with the smile of a delightful dark-haired young lady. She handed me the coin, I returned her smile and mouthed my thanks.

Nothing odd there you may think, but as I locked eyes with this damsel I realised that things were not as they once were. There was the day when such an exchange between male and female would be one of assessment; male thinking words to the effect: "Coo, she's nice! I wonder if…", while the female is thinking: "Humph. I know what he's thinking – mind you, he has got a nice…"

Anyway, I became aware that her smile was not one of evaluation but an almost melancholy look tinged with sympathy as she helped this poor old chap retrieve his money, doubtless dropped from hands that are no longer as steady as they once were.

Needless to say, she achieved the perpendicular before me and was well on her way by the time I straightened up.

Ah, straightening up. As I headed back to work I vowed to sharpen up and words uttered all too frequently by the ever vigilant Mrs Haverson echoed in my mind. "You're getting a real stoop. It makes you look old!"

I snapped my spine into place, forced my shoulders back, sucked in my stomach and strode on my way. I must have looked like someone grappling with a severe tropical disease, desperately attempting to contain the onset of a serious explosion of the bowels.

But, as you make your way towards the twilight years, it's a tricky call as to when you let go of some of the aspects of life that belong to those of a more tender age. Certain pubs become no go areas; they're full of body pierced individuals wearing ripped jeans, gulping lager from the bottle.

You look sadly out of place ordering a pint of bitter – in a mug – and a packet of pork scratchings.

And talking of jeans, when do you stop wearing fashion jeans; the ones with the faded knees and bum and wrinkly fronts?

And what about trainers? Does something with a fluorescent Nike tick look out of place on a foot that's shuffling along in the Post Office queue?

The lady who cuts my hair is forever trying to persuade me to have a more trendy style. Can you imagine what comments that would cause when I walked into work?

"Aye aye; what's he up to? No good I'll be bound. I've often wondered where he dashes off to at lunchtime."

But why should we grow old gracefully? Make a statement, be the oldest swinger in town.

But are you sure about that gold medallion?

Old dogs and new tricks

Every now and again reports on the proposal that drivers of 70-plus years should take another test. Hmm... I remember my original driving test and I'm not sure I'd want to go through it again.

There was no theory test when I earned my wheels, other than a couple of questions on the Highway Code. Here I was extremely fortunate. Having not long left school anything that involved my head in a book had been consigned to oblivion; time spent revising the Highway Code was short.

Like taking my GCEs, the night before the test I panicked and attempted to cram my memory full of knowledge.

By the time I got to the test centre I had road signs swirling around in my head, facts and figures merged. My brain was on overload. Bizarrely, the only thing I could remember was the stopping distance at 60mph.

I had a lesson prior to the test. It did not go well. According to my instructor, I wasn't looking in my mirror enough and the tone of his voice clearly indicated that he was looking forward to further income from me.

I can't remember the test itself. I do recall him banging his clipboard on the dashboard for the emergency stop and I have a fleeting memory of a body wracked with tension as I tried to look over my shoulder to reverse around a corner.

Back at the test centre I drew the car to a halt, applied the handbrake, switched off the engine and unclamped sweaty hands from the steering wheel. Then the memory again becomes blurred until the final question.

"What is the stopping distance at 60mph?"

Yes, oh yes!

"Two hundred and forty feet," I squeaked in a voice that was bordering on hysteria. It was the only fact I had memorised.

I recall the examiner's final words with great clarity.

"That's all Mr Haverson. You've passed your test." Then, as he wrote out the prized pink slip, he added: "Is your Dad still in the police force? I served with him until I retired. Do give him my regards."

I know what you're thinking, but no, I'm sure that played no part in me passing.

My instructor walked up.

"Con…grat…u…lations!" he boomed. It seemed to take ages for him to get the word out. But he was beaming broadly. A success to his credit outweighed the loss of further tuition fees.

But it's what happened next that I find intriguing in the light of the purge on older drivers.

Within an hour I had become a qualified driver; licensed to be in charge of a chunk of speeding metal. And within a further hour I was making my first solo flight.

John, a colleague, walked into the office, threw me the keys to the company Mini and said: "Just drive me to the garage to pick up my car."

The journey there was fine, but on the way back I was terrified. Having been accompanied every time I was behind the wheel, suddenly I was alone in this huge cabin with a steering wheel up one corner.

And it was only a Mini!

No one to ask at junctions: "Can I nip out or should I wait?" I had to make the decision.

I made it back to the office – and then I had to park. I staggered into the office and sank into the chair at my desk. John had long since been back and I mumbled something about traffic.

Gradually I became accustomed to being on my own in the car, confidence grew and the right foot became heavier. And this is where the debate comes in. Is a cocky 18-year-old with swift reactions safer than a 70-year-old with ingrained habits who is not so sharp with the brakes?

But here's a suggestion. If it's felt that 70-year-olds need to be retested, how about some form of review for youngsters say, two years after they passed their test, with the option to put them back on a provisional licence if they fail?

The trouble is, everybody thinks they're a good driver.

But how many know the stopping distance at 60mph?

A Claus in his contract

Santa leaned against the sleigh and sighed. "Why can't it be like the old days?" he mused. "All I had to do was load the presents, turf my little helpers out of their bunks, harness the reindeer and away."

Life had been difficult for the poor old chap. He'd just had a CRB check to make sure he was okay to work with the elves; Elf & Safety had ordered him to install lower steps so the elves had easy access to their hut.

The elves weren't supposed to be there. They turned up one Friday night and by Monday they had built a hut, laid down tarmac and connected water.

And Defra had chosen the day before Christmas Eve to inspect the stables to renew his reindeer licence.

He'd had to carry out a risk assessment for going down chimneys. It took five hours to fill in the form. Why did they want to know his mother's maiden name, for goodness sake?

Then the council had fined him because one of the elves had put the remains of the wrapping paper in the wrong wheelie bin. And now he was being sued because he had shouted at the perpetrator, calling him a "Stupid little elf".

The elf reported him, saying he was grossly offended and traumatised at being called "little". He claimed it was demeaning; he had hardly slept and was having nightmares.

Santa couldn't quite work that one out.

On top of it all he had no idea how he was going to fit in all the deliveries. Thanks to the European Working Time Directive he only had half the usual time to get around the world.

Santa sighed again and carried on loading. Just sorting the presents had been a chore this year. All the Action Men had been repainted pink and labelled Action Persons to conform to Harriet Harman's** equality laws.

And he'd been lobbied by the union not to use any toys from Third World sweatshops.

Oh well, he thought, it's only once a year – although Brussels was planning to issue a directive that Christmas should be moved to mid-summer's day. They had been promised a referendum on it, but the prime minister said it was only "tidying up" the previous proposal that Easter should be moved to

October.

Just then, Rudolph appeared.

"We've had a meeting," he announced pompously, "and we have a demand. My members want a guarantee there'll be regular stops for breaks. We're refusing to pull the sleigh for more than four hours at a time. We'll be keeping an eye on the tachograph."

It was at this point that Santa almost gave up. Then he had an idea. Why didn't he order everything over the internet, from Amazon? Have it all gift wrapped and sent direct to homes. That would cut his costs. No reindeer to feed and keep. Those wretched elves could all be made redundant – let them find out what life is like on Jobseeker's Allowance.

No more compensation claims for dislodged chimney pots. No more expensive drugs to treat Rudolph's nose. He'd had to pay since NICE had ruled it wasn't cost effective to prescribe them on the National Elf.

And he could get rid of the sleigh. If he did it through the scrappage scheme he'd be able to get a nice two-seater for him and Mrs Claus.

This cheered Santa up enormously. He had a plan!

As he returned to his labours, the postman arrived. The mail used to arrive before breakfast; these days it turned up mid-afternoon. He jabbed his thumb into a suspicious-looking brown envelope.

Damn speed cameras! He'd been caught doing 31mph in a 30mph limit over Westminster. Three more points on his licence; next time it would be an automatic ban, then who'd deliver the presents?

Just then two official looking gentlemen came up the drive.

"Mr Claus?" they asked.

"Yeeesss," replied Santa warily.

"We've had a report that you are using a ladder to load your sleigh. We have no record of you being ladder trained. How are you with heights?"

* Sometime after publication a lady picked up the magazine in the hairdressers. She rang me to say it was so funny she must have a copy. I found one in the cupboard and sent it to her.

Around the same time a parish magazine from Amersham, Bucks contacted me to ask permission to reproduce it.

The reaction reassured me that people were fed up with all the red tape and political correctness.

Progress to the next queue

I have an up and over garage door. Needless to say, it's been some years since I opened it to put the car away. As for many people, my garage has become a mini warehouse. The garage door has weathered over the years and, I confess, I have not painted it as regularly as I should. Well, it's a tedious job. Getting rid of flaking paint and rust; grime gets in the grooves and they are quite cumbersome to paint.

But now, the mechanism is nearing the end of its life and it needs replacing. I have been casting around for a uPVC door, one that is maintenance-free.

Mrs Haverson piped up that one or two people she knew had installed new garage doors – with a remote control.

She moves in different circles to me. But I think an automatic door is a step too far. I made a speech about still being able to stagger out of the car to open it. Besides, what would the neighbours think when I appeared in the drive, pushed a button and stood there grandly, watching it rise like a portcullis to reveal an embarrassing stash of furniture, boxes and bikes that will probably never again fulfil their purpose in society.

Use of technology can go a bit too far. Okay, I'm sure, like me, many of you remember the days before the photocopier? Messy old carbon paper and those awful Gestetner machines for running off duplicate documents.

I would not want to return to those days; but I do think, in some areas, so-called progress is being imposed on us under the guise of better service when the basic motive is to cut costs. I can manage self-scanning at a supermarket – just; but I prefer to go to a human being on a till.

But I got a real shock when I ventured into the main Post Office in Norwich recently. Last time I visited, there was a long queue, but the welcome cry of "Cashier number three please" was pretty constant and I soon got served.

This time, I was confronted with a screen, a large board of instructions and an even larger gentleman who was on hand to offer guidance – and quell protests.

The gist of it is this: The screen has a number of options; you press the button for the service you require; take a ticket with a number on it, like you would at the supermarket deli; and wait to be summoned.

Where the queue used to snake around the room, there are now some sofas. It was like the waiting room at the hospital; a sea of bewildered and anxious faces waiting for the consultant to call them.

"Number 265 to cash point L," says a silky voice. You have to react pretty smartish to find your designated window.

As I walked in, the screen "minder" inquired: "How can we help you today sir?"

I proffered a letter and stammered that all I wanted to do was post it to America.

"You can use the coin-operated machine for that to save you queuing. The young woman there will help you," he replied, directing me to a, well, queue.

This, I discovered, is called Post & Go. Here, the young woman was trying to educate a poor technologically challenged individual on how to weigh a packet, choose the speed of dispatch and insert his coins.

I waited with a few others. They looked rather soulful, as if they had just missed the last bus.

After a while, I aborted my mission with a view to going back later.

I didn't.

Where will it all end? Perhaps one day you will go to the doctor's surgery and be faced with a screen. Displayed on it will be a list of illnesses. "Press button for symptoms." Then you'll be asked to choose more options.

"How often does the diarrhoea strike?"

"Have you had a hot curry lately?"

"Please wait while Dr Terminal diagnoses your symptoms."

"Dr Terminal's recommended treatment: do not stray too far from home for 24 hours."

Let's Talk magazine, August, 2010

Perils of the health MOT

Just what do you say when a young, blonde, female doctor looks you straight in the eye and says: "How about a rectal examination then?" I was having a health assessment and medicine woman had just peered into my ears to establish the wax factor when she made this quantum leap to a more sensitive part of the body.

Shocked into honesty, I blurted out:

"I had one four years ago."

"Right," she said. "Better do one now then."

It's one of those things where the anticipation is worse than the actual event, though I was glad when it was over.

I've had these health check-ups for a few years and I'm glad I do. Usually, I am supremely confident until the day; then every cough, twinge and ache becomes magnified in to a set of terminal symptoms.

However, as you get older time gets more precious and if you need to do something to prolong active life, you should bite the bullet and do it. That, I admit, is a case of do what I say, not what I do.

I emerged from the medical with a slapped wrist for my weight. Coupled to this was a warning that the ratio of my waist measurement to my height is out of kilter, putting me in the red zone. Immediately I vowed that portions at mealtimes would be reduced. Anything containing too much saturated fat would not pass my lips. My cherished pints of beer would be rationed. Besides, forbidden fruits and all that, it would be something to look forward to. Make it taste even better.

I recall the time I was hooked up to the ECG. The nurse pressed the start button and after the machine had been scratching away for about 30 seconds she cried out: "Oh no!"

I froze with horror. This was it. Okay, give it to me straight.

"Damn thing's not working properly, we'll have to start again," she exclaimed.

Phew!

It's surprising how vulnerable you feel at times like this. While waiting for Doctor Digit to do her examination, I sat in the waiting room reflecting on the previous few months, convincing myself that I hadn't done too badly. In fact I was in pretty good condition. After all, Mrs Haverson makes sure I have a decent diet and get my five-a-day.

Veg that is, not pints.

While it could have been much worse, I do have to take action to combat the increase in weight. As well as avoiding fatty foods, I was urged to take more exercise.

I was told: "Do 20 minutes exercise which raises the heart rate three times a week and you can lose a stone in a year – and eat normally."

Well, you should see me erupt from the Let's Talk office at lunchtime and walk vigorously around the shops. That takes at least 20 minutes. Goodness knows what they make of that on the CCTV cameras.

"Hello, here he comes again. He looks like Groucho Marx."

I don't use lifts or escalators. Maybe sometimes there is the odd crisp or peanut too many consumed in front of the telly. But a chap's got to have a treat now and again.

I mow the lawn, dig the garden; a few calories lost there. And clambering into the loft takes aerobics to a new level.

But who am I kidding? Getting fit has to be taken seriously. Activity in our daily lives is not sufficient to keep us in trim. I need to focus; discipline myself. Yes, I know you with long memories will remind me that I was going regularly to the gym. Well, it was doing me good but I could take no more pounding mind-numbingly away on the treadmill.

I have a fitness DVD, which is quite fun to do. Though I'm not sure what the neighbours think when the curtains close on a Saturday afternoon and there is the sound of heavy breathing from within.

Oh, that reminds me. There was no problem with the prostate.

Thanks for asking.

Let's Talk magazine, October, 2010

I'm getting good at all these 21st Century languages

In my continuing battle to become a fully paid-up member of the 21st century, I am pleased to say I have made some progress. I am now sending text messages without punctuation. Okay, I do still spell out all the words, but I am working on that. In addition, I have finally succeeded in introducing the word 'cool' into my vocabulary; don't use it a lot but in appropriate company I slip it in to show I'm seriously with it.

But probably my greatest achievement in modernising myself happened last month. Someone asked: "How are you today, Neil?" and I replied: "I'm good."

How cool is that!

None of your "Very well thank you." Or: "Got a bit of a cold actually."
Modern parlance, straight from the hip.

And "I'm good," also means "No thank you".

"Wanna another drink?"

"I'm good."

Alternatively you can decline like this.

"Want some more coffee?"

"No, you're all right."

Don't use words like 'fantastic', things are 'wicked', and if somebody does something that's a bit off the wall, it's 'random'.

Slip those into conversation when it goes quiet in the pub and you'll gain real respect. I am desperately looking for someone I can call a chav. But since I don't really know what one is I'm treading very carefully.

It's when I get in this cynical mood that Mrs Haverson scoffs: "Pathetic! You sound really old when you say things like that."

I suppose, as ever, she has a point. I think back to my younger days and the things we did and said. I remember my father's horror at that new dance that swept the country. It was called the Twist. I still have in my mind a gruesome image of him attempting to do it.

And our language must have been equally as bewildering to him as today's jargon is to us. I had a forage to remind me of the words we used when we were hepcats; drinking Coke, not snorting it, hitching lifts and not boy racers in souped up GTis and the only wine we experienced was in gums, not bottles.

First thing I realised, of course, was that 'cool' is a Fifties word, so I've reintroduced it to my vocabulary rather than discovered it. But some of the others I came across sound like a foreign language today. When we had some 'bread' we put on our 'threads' and went to the 'flicks'. In the Sixties everything was 'groovy' and as the drugs and protest culture gained momentum, life became a 'drag', occasionally it was a 'gas' and we urged people to have 'peace man'.

And yes, when I derided their communication skills, I expect my children looked at me with as much disdain as I did at my father. I thought he was 'square'. I daren't think what my offspring thought – or probably still think – of me. Mind you, my son and his mates used to describe an attractive girl as 'fit', which I suppose is a bit more flattering than the Sixties 'Bit of stuff' or 'Bit of totty'.

The trouble is words slip so quickly into conversation they subsequently find their way into the Oxford Dictionary. Since the South African World Cup, Vuvuzela, that noisy South African instrument, is officially part of the English language. And thanks to the credit crunch that ugly word, Staycation, is also listed.

You just can't fight it.

Oh well, stick another tanner in the juke box dude and let's have a blast.

The Last Word

In frank exchanges with our partners we chaps rarely have the last word. Well, perhaps that's not strictly true. We have two last words; yes dear.

But I have been in rather a privileged position. Thanks to the Fortress H column I can have the final says; lay matters to rest in print.

There have been times when Mrs H and I have had words and I have ended up apologising even though I have no idea what I've done wrong. But the next Saturday, I can put my point of view without fear of contradiction. Thus gaining sympathy from those also dwelling under the thumb while irking the female readers.

I should add that I have offered the column to Mrs H on more than one occasion to put her side of the story. She scoffs: "I'm no good with words."

That from a woman who can catch me with my hand in the biscuit tin and, barely pausing for breath, unleash a lengthy lecture on the damage I am doing to my body by consuming too much sugar.

Women often say to me: "Does my husband write your column", while men ask: "Are you married to my wife?"

In a way I find that most reassuring. It tells me that what goes on at Fortress H is mirrored in so many households. As I recount the latest tale of marital bliss I know it's happening in your house too.

We all live in a Fortress H.

Neil
Haverson

Running repairs pose a problem

The Fortress laundry service has been restored with the washing machine back in working order.

Now there is a blockage in the sewing department.

I remember this happened many years ago when we were first married. It was the lining of a mac as I recall. When the repaired garment failed to materialise, I, being a brave new husband, sent Mrs H a tongue-in-cheek memo requesting that my mac be given some priority as it was the rainy season.

There followed what was to become a familiar lecture on the hapless lot of the modern housewife, but the repair was done.

There was a minor blip recently. I began to thank Mrs H for buying me a new shirt. Then I realised that the shirt looked vaguely familiar. It transpired that it was one that had been submitted some months before to have a button sewn on and I had forgotten all about it. She claimed the delay was due to the fact that she had lost the button.

Before I am accused of being a typical useless male, yes, I can sew a button on. They don't stay on for long, but I can do it. Anyway, every time I offer, Mrs H insists on doing it. This is because she thinks it is her job as "the little woman," as she sometimes refers to herself.

Now there has been another sewing delay that rivals the incident of the legendary pair of trousers that went in to be turned up. Two years later they emerged untouched and, miraculously, they fitted. With that protracted experience in mind, I decided to send

fortress H

neil haverson

Neil's flushed with embarrassment exploring a new shopping centre and even the ladies' loos...

I HAD ONE OF THOSE MOMENTS the other day when I was confronted with a situation for which the brain simply can't come up with a solution. A feeling of mild panic wells up in the pit of the stomach and the mind crunches options like someone playing a fruit machine in search of that elusive jackpot.

My desperate situation occurred in the new Chapelfield development last week. The whole issue of this new shopping centre is bad news for any husband. There are now so many shops in Norwich that, what for me is a fractious marital trawl, could be something that travel agents offer as a short break.

Mrs H decided that we would carry out a reconnaissance of the potential credit card swiping that was available in the new centre. It was to be a swift tour on the understanding that she would blitz the place at a later date with her goss 'n' shop mate while I remained within the confines of Fortress H doing chaps things like painting skirting boards.

Our journey of discovery started out well as we joined masses of people purposefully marching what appeared to be nowhere. As is the case with Mrs H and me, the smell of freshly-brewed coffee lassoed us and we were soon taking caffeine on board to sustain us through the rest of Mrs H's reconnoitre.

Inevitably, after a large coffee, the loo was the next thing on the agenda. There are strict rules here. We can't both go at once. One of us has to play minder to the carrier bags while the other seeks relief. Mrs H went first. When she emerged, she informed me that, if I went in a cubicle, the locks were stiff with newness.

"I nearly panicked!" she said. "If a girl in there hadn't warned me I'd have been really worried."

I breezed into the loo. There were two cubicles, one engaged. I dived, so to speak, into the other. I was just about press the flush when something made me freeze. I could hear the sound of voices; female voices.

It took just a nano second to register. So that's why there were no urinals. I was in the ladies.

At this point the brain reclassified the situation from routine to utter terror. I bought a bit of time by delaying pressing the flush. In what seemed like hours but was probably only 15 seconds, I wracked my confused brain for a solution. Nothing rational came to me.

Perhaps they'd just go away. Unlikely. Perhaps whoever was in the other cubicle would come out and the rest would go en mass into it and I could slip away.

Should I use my mobile to contact Mrs H and summon her to my rescue? But what would she say? "Excuse me, my husband's in there. Do you mind if he comes out?"

Besides, there was no signal.

The female chatter continued. I knew there was nothing for it; I had to face it out. I flushed the loo, took a deep breath and burst out of the door. I was greeted by two ladies who, I have to say, looked decidedly unfazed to see a male erupt from their loos.

"Ha ha! I'm in the wrong loo!" I practically shrieked with hysteria. Then I thought, if in doubt, blame Mrs H. "I'm awfully sorry, my wife said go in and turn left. I did and here I am," I continued in a voice a good octave above the norm.

Fortunately, they just giggled. And I didn't give them time to reply as I crashed Tom and Jerry-style through the door. I sought sanctuary in the proper gents where I swiftly washed my hands. I zoomed back to Mrs H.

"Grab the bags quick!" I hissed. "Let's get out of here before those ladies come out of the loo."

High on adrenalin, I led a bewildered Mrs H into the crowds. She must have wondered what on earth I had done. When I thought it was safe, I stopped and related my experience to her. She did, of course, think it a great hoot but reversed my falling stress levels by speculating what might have happened if the ladies had not seen the funny side.

At that point my mobile rang. What! Had they tracked me down? But it was Brat Major, as ever wondering if we were anywhere near a shop and if so could we just get...

I was still not fully in control and before I knew it I had blurted out the story to her. I realised that was a mistake as knowledge of my plight was no longer contained and, no doubt, in the retelling, the story would receive some embellishment.

I was more or less calm by the time we arrived home. Brat Major was just leaving Fortress H accompanied by Spoilerman.

"I hear the toilets in Chapelfield are a bit dodgy," he mused.

Hmm, nothing wrong with the toilets; just those who use them. Mind you, perhaps they could make those pictures on the doors a bit bigger. ∎

Neil's latest collection of classic columns, Fortress H: Reigning Brats and Mogs, is now available from all good bookshops and Archant offices, priced at £6.99.

Wonders to see in my time machine

by **Neil Haverson**   neil.haverson@archant.co.uk

Picture: THINKSTOCK

There is a rather handy facility on a computer. Should something go wrong, like one of those wretched viruses infects your machine, you can travel back in time and restore the operating system of your computer to a date and time before the problem occurred – without losing any of the work you've done in the meantime.

I had to restore my computer recently for this very reason. I couldn't help thinking how useful it would be if this could be applied to our lives.

I mean, suppose you felt a nasty bout of the 'flu coming on, wouldn't it be good if you could restore your body to the condition it was before you caught the bug, but, as with the computer, nothing else was affected. You still had that good night out with the lads or that romantic candlelit dinner with a loved one.

I'm warming to this idea. What if I forgot my wedding anniversary? I could restore things to the day before and order some flowers. Or go back to the day before the Grand National and back the winner.

The reverse occurred to me while I was trawling through my memories for the Fifties feature on Page 34. It focussed me on how things have progressed in leaps and bounds. Maybe "progressed" isn't the right word. It could be argued that not everything has changed for the better.

But do an H G Wells and imagine a time machine in, say, the 1800s. I suspect someone living then would have their mind blown if they landed on what they knew as the high street in their tiny village to find it in the 21st Century teaming with polluting horseless carriages, women in short skirts and men without hats, ties and waistcoats.

> 'What if I forgot my wedding anniversary? I could restore things to the day before and order some flowers'

The butchers, bakers and grocers had gone, and in its place was something called Lidl.

And what on earth are those giant metal birds in the sky?

It would all be too much to comprehend. Mind you, suppose we could hop aboard a time machine and fast forward a couple of hundred years, I wonder what we'd find. Last month I mentioned the futuristic ideas on Star Trek. Well, there'd probably be no traffic – beam me up Scotty would have become a reality. Similarly, Lidl will have gone in favour of ordering Sunday lunch by speaking into a transmitter and the food manifesting itself on the dining table.

Or perhaps roast beef, Yorkshire pud and all the trimmings will be compressed in a pill so a romantic dinner consists of swallowing a tablet by candlelight.

It's hard to imagine that technology and our way of life will advance in the future as rapidly as it has in the past 50 years. We live and work in the moment and, thankfully, can't see into the future.

The first TVs were revolutionary. Who would have dreamt that in 60 years' time there would be huge flat screens in full colour high definition?

In George Orwell's 1984 there were screens in homes where Big Brother kept an eye on the citizens. Already the latest Smart TVs have built in wifi and webcams. Apparently, hackers can not only monitor what you watch but take control of the webcam and actually spy on you in your living room.

At present there is nothing you can do to block it. It's frightening.

Oh Scotty please, beam me up!

■ **Read previous editions of The Last Word at www.letstalk24.co.uk**